Selected Poems

D1564822

First published in 2012 by
Liberties Press
7 Rathfarnham Road | Terenure | Dublin 6w
Tel: +353 (1) 405 5701
www.libertiespress.com | info@libertiespress.com

Trade enquiries to Gill & Macmillan Distribution
Hume Avenue | Park West | Dublin 12
T: +353 (1) 500 9534 | F: +353 (1) 500 9595 | E: sales@gillmacmillan.ie

Distributed in the UK by
Turnaround Publisher Services
Unit 3 | Olympia Trading Estate | Coburg Road | London N22 6TZ
T: +44 (0) 20 8829 3000 | E: orders@turnaround-uk.com

Distributed in the United States by
Dufour Editions | PO Box 7 | Chester Springs | Pennsylvania | 19425

Copyright © Moyra Donaldson, 2012

The author has asserted her moral rights.

ISBN: 978-1-907593-52-9
2 4 6 8 10 9 7 5 3 1
A CIP record for this title is available from the British Library.

Cover design by Sin É Design
Internal design by Liberties Press
Printed by Bell & Bain Ltd

This book is sold subject to the condition that it shall not, by way
of trade or otherwise, be lent, resold, hired out or otherwise circulated,
without the publisher's prior consent, in any form other than that in
which it is published and without a similar condition including this
condition being imposed on the subsequent publisher.

No part of this publication may be reproduced or transmitted in any
form or by any means, electronic or mechanical, including
photocopying, recording or storage in any information or retrieval
system, without the prior permission of the publisher in writing.

The publishers gratefully acknowledge
financial assistance from the Arts Council and the Arts Council
of Northern Ireland.

Selected Poems

Moyra Donaldson

For John, Claire and Jannah

Contents

from *Beneath the Ice* (2001)

from *Miracle Fruit* (2010)

Foreword

I have admired Moyra Donaldson's work for a number of years. Now, her *Selected Poems* brings together work from her four previous collections and amounts to a wonderful achievement.

Donaldson is a poet of disappointed and enduring love, and dark and fantastical dreams. *Snakeskin Stilettos*, her first collection, is full of haunting poems populated by characters from fairytales, folktales and mythology, including Snow White, Rapunzel, an Irish Dervish, Leda and a bearded old satyr. An erotic charge pulsates through her work too. Her love poems are filled with pain and longing; the eponymous snakeskin stilettos of her first collection are 'forbidden and dangerous'.

If 'It is a kind of courage/ to hear only what is said' ('Poisoned Glen'), then it takes a different kind of courage to 'grow a new tongue' ('Exile') and articulate the dream-world of the imagination.

As the title *Beneath the Ice* suggests, much of Donaldson's second book happens below the surface, behind facades and in the darker regions of the psyche, in the shadow corners of myth and folk-tale. Drawing images from the sub-conscious, Donaldson's muse is shape-changing and mercurial where 'she has/ made the past no place/ but substance of her flesh/ flesh of my dreams.'

Born in Bangor, County Down, Donaldson does not write about the Troubles in any overt way. She admits that they may have influenced her psyche. I don't suppose her Presbyterian upbringing has infiltrated her poetic vision much either, other than in distant echoes of the bible. Revealingly in an interview with John Brown, from In The Chair, Donaldson admits to 'discovering the influence of absences at Queen's University.' A poet who was put off writing during her time at university in Belfast in the mid to late 1970s,

Donaldson returned to writing poetry in her thirties. Her approach by then was crystallised by a kind of vatic vision fed by the pool of images drawn from the unconscious.

Her third collection book , *The Horse's Nest* is a book filled with magic, where a kind of folkloric consciousness creates poems with lines which could have come from riddles, spells and curses. Often, the tone of Donaldson's poetry is wry, ironic, melancholic and seductive:

> Last night she dreamt the glass
> was broken and the tiny creatures
> loose, escaped around her head,
> a blur of wings, ruby throats
> and stabbing beaks.
> She tried to shoosh them away,
> flapping her hands, but they flew
> into her hair, her eyes, her mouth.

> from 'The Hummingbird Case'

Donaldson's voice is a quiet one, full of integrity and mystery and *The Horse's Nest* is a book again of dreams, but of elegy too. There is a beautiful sequence about the passing of her mother called 'Cheyne-Stokes Breathing', and 'The Hummingbird Case' is one of several sequences where Donaldson's lyric power gains momentum with an almost nightmarish fever. Like Auden, Donaldson's argument is implicit, 'every poem is to be rooted in imaginative awe.'

The lighter side of Donaldson's work includes wry portraits of 'Bangor Girls 1960s', and 'When I am Old', but her humour is invariably black: see 'A free lunch or Ulster says no.'

The surrealistic vein in Donaldson's work is both startling and compelling. The poem 'Nest' is a surreal evocation of a series of potent mythological and sub-conscious symbols:

> My horse is waiting, shaded and patient
> his skin is comfort, his breath green
> as he carries me on his back

to the flat stone altar at the forest's heart.
Being dead, I lay myself down on it,
thankfully, and the black bird comes,
lifts me to her round high nest.

In a Poetry Ireland reading at the Unitarian Church in Dublin in 2006, Donaldson commented that the poem was a form of healing. It's clear that the current definition of a horse's nest or its homonym mare's nest as something which is in a mess, or something found which seems first like treasure but is actually an illusion, is not quite the same horse's nest as the one Donaldson portrays. More interesting is perhaps Robert Graves's discussion in The White Goddess of poets and gleemen. He anticipates criticism from scholars on his 'preposterous group of mare's nests', to go on to ask what is a mare's nest anyway. Quoting Shakespeare 'who substitutes St. Swithold for Odin, the original hero of the ballad, his mare's nest becomes quite literally a Night Mare - one of the cruellest aspects of the White Goddess. Her nests when one comes across them in dreams, lodged in clefts or the branches of enormous hollow yews, are built of carefully chosen twigs, lined with white-horse hair and the plumage of prophetic birds and littered with the jaw-bones and entrails of poets. The prophet Job said of her: 'She dwelleth and abideth on the rock. Her young ones also suck up blood.'

In 'Nest', Donaldson finds herself quite literally 'inside the egg.' The transformations she experiences in the poem take her from cell to creator until the final moments when:

My horse is waiting
bright and patient:
his skin is sunlight
and his breath air.
Amongst the moss his bones
are white and dry.

In my beak, I lift
his great rib hull

his long leg bones,
the instrument of his skull,

and in the highest branches
of the tallest tree
in wind tossed waves of leaves,
I build my horse's nest, my ship of bones.

Here is a poet who becomes not the stuff of the nest, but its maker. Invoking, possibly intuitively, a collective image like the horse's nest charges Donaldson's work with a current both mysterious and alluring.

In her fourth book, *Miracle Fruit*, Donaldson's work develops the carnivalesque chimera further with poems inspired by the Scottish surgeon John Hunter and a visit to The Hunterian Society of London. Donaldson's work here is amplified by her historical curiosity and the many voices she assumes.

If there are political subtexts in Donaldson's work they are subtle. In 'Old Gods in the British Museum', we are told that some of the gods 'have forgotten almost what it was to be feared.' Bakhtin's notion of the grotesque body and the carnival help us to see Donaldson's poetry as more public. The 'man-bear' or 'pig-faced woman' suggest a regenerative spectacle before the final 'dissolution of the circus' where the ponies are sold to a riding school 'where they soon forget their tricks.' Even so, it's still not possible for us to forget, from Donaldson's first collection, the image of the poet's hooves dissolving beneath her school desk after play-time has ended. *Selected Poems* will transport you too to a magical place.

Paul Perry
July 2012

from *Snakeskin Stilettos*

(1998)

Exile

What ground is mine
if I would govern myself?
Where is my country
if neither bogs nor gantries
speak of me?
Where can I stand
if I am not one thing
or the other?

My grandfather knew where he stood.
Ancestors planted his feet
in fertile soil, green futures were
named in his name, possessed.
He preached their flinty faith
in mission tents, visions of eternal life
on soft Ulster evenings,

but there was no redemption.
Not in the land, or through the Blood.
Not in the hard lessons of duty, obedience,
with which he marked his children.

He is stripped of virtue,
his legacy a stone
of no magic, no transcendence.
No children ever turn to swans,
wafer remains wafer on the tongue,
and flesh is always flesh.

My two white birds will bring me
water from the mountains,
beakfuls of sweet sips.
I will grow a new tongue,

paint my body with circles
and symbols of strength, mark myself
as one who belongs in the desert.

Astronomy

Like Gulliver, I lie immobilised, but yet
content to let the moss grow on my limbs and sides.
Tendrils of ferns unfurl before and through my eyes,
my head is full of buds – so though I do regret
the loss of much – here in this place so much remains.
Besides, freedom is treacherous, for even when
you tread with care, not trusting eyes to know for sure
what's solid ground, or what's just air, your heart retains
the memory of the drop, the letting down.
Now I'm so still that small birds make their nests in me.
I watch the stars move in their paths above my head.
Almost content. So far below, and closely bound.

Thinking about autumn

I was looking at the garden
and thinking about autumn
and how I just can't like it
despite the colours of leaves
dahlias fat ripe elderberries
blackberries hips and haws
because it means winter's coming
and I don't like winter
despite how snow looks
on the trees I can see
from my kitchen window
frosty night stars
big fires and hot whiskeys
then I thought maybe I
should just learn
to content myself
because after all
it's the nature of things
and after winter there is
always spring and I love spring
the way may blossom is unbelievably
white and everything is bursting out
growing reaching moving
into lovely lovely summer
sun and bare skin
long light and short hot nights
then I saw the birds
lined up on the telephone lines
ready for leaving and I thought
screw contentment
if I had wings I'd go too.

Mother who has been

my broken bowl   my holy grail
my long silence   my spoken truth
my tiny bound feet   my seven league boots
my never quite   my every first prize

when you come on the forgotten well among the trees
lower the bucket, hand over hand: the rope will hold
as you draw up the cold clear water. Feel how it cools
your blood's wild fire, scorched earth greens back, seeds burst,
and you can read again the hieroglyphics of branches
budding across the sky. Birds wake to fly and small animals
uncurl among the nascent ferns. Listen –
a child's untroubled voice rings on the morning air, singing
as you fetch water for your mother from the wood well

and nothing will be lost.
Here is your father, once the youngest boy
neighbours had ever seen between
the handles of a plough, the hardest worker.
He lies under my heart carved in stone,
grown to the man who never wept.
Soft as a breast, your mother
is my children's remembered dream of milky mouths.
Each thought undone, each memory unpeeled,
each year of you, I fold, hold to my cheek
like the white linen your grandmother sewed
by candlelight. I breathe you in, the living skin of me
knowing it was always too late for us, for everything
happens as it must, in its own moment.

As I become the past on which the future rests,
forgiveness is a final irrelevance.
Years from now, on some perfect summer evening,

I will look and you'll be in the garden, gathering fruit.
A small dog will follow at your heels

as you pick gooseberries, bursting juice,
strawberries red ripe under leaves.
When you see me, you will beckon me to come,
and I'll run down the years into your arms.

Visits

She's quite content today,
chatting with Margaret and Meta,
but I am struggling.
What does it signify,
their conversation?
A raggle of crows
blown sideways in an east wind
across a flat canvas, a flat sky,
a world without horizons.
In this new landscape
I am still the outsider,
the only one who thinks it matters –
perspective, the earth's curve.

She wants to go home
to where her mother is waiting
by the first shining hearth.
She wants to go home
as a child can ache
for love forever.

She knows I'm not a stranger,
the family face familiar still:
a sister perhaps?
I crouch, dreaming
behind a latticework of words –
red lips, blood
spilling from a bowl,
dark stains of unconsciousness.

She moves away from me
down the corridor,
just a strange old woman
scuttling along,
bent on her own business,
nothing to do with me at all.

A modest ghost

My father is a modest ghost, undramatic,
not given to walking the long night watches,
or taking up a chair at family parties.
Rather, he appears from the spaces
between things, connections made,
inconspicuous moments tumbling
into consciousness as if by accident.
I have glimpsed his reflection in the
iridescent feathers of a pheasant,
startled in the early morning fields,
gone as soon as look.
A perfect note, held to breath's end,
is the touch of his hand.

He's pleased I notice him, and understand.

12.05 AM New Year's Day

Church bells chime the change,
and the new is rung in.
As the ground glitters with frost
so does the sky with stars,
and I am standing somewhere in between,
guessing at constellations,
trying to sense the ancient imagination
that saw and named them.
I hear your voice, reciting the Catechism,
questions and answers.
I close my eyes, and see the nebulae
of blood vessels, the galaxies of nerves,
the imploded shadows inside your head;
black holes down which you flow
as space and time distorts.
I watch but cannot follow,
and you are almost out of sight already,
approaching the singularity,
moving beyond answers.

What she might pray

No matter how far I have drifted,
even if land is nowhere to be seen,
do not let the sea completely own me.
I could not bear to hear no other rhythm
but the tide's relentlessness.
Do not abandon me. Anchor me with love.

Watcher

When there is nothing left but shadow,
I will sit with you
under the December evening sky,
under its red and black disintegration,
until even the mountains, cutting
their perfect shapes across our horizon,
are subsumed into night.

Side ward

Wrapped up neatly in the past tense
by busy nieces and their families,
I wait. My nights have become endless.
Footsteps in the corridor, machinery's hum,
my fingers rustling like paper on the sheets.
Mornings have shrunk to a medicinal routine.
The thermometer placed between my dry lips,
blood pressure, catheter checked.
Needles pushed beneath translucent skin.
I try to remember when my body
was a private thing, closed.
Spiralling in and out of thinnest sleep,
the pictures come, scenes and faces
from the past hanging in air.
What was, what might have been.
Fact, impression, dream.
The difference hardly seems to matter any more.
No one remains to hear the telling of my years,
like beads unstrung they scatter, roll away.
This odour of decay I smell on my own breath
repels all visitors, except the ghosts –
and only nurses hold my hand, or call me love.

Hibernating

Store what you may need again,
bonfire the worn out, the outgrown,
then slow – midwinter's rhythm.
Enter a dreamless time,
and delta-wave deep,
sleep out the past.
Do not wake
until the sun across your eyelids
promises a world of light.

Poems for four children

If I climb high enough, to where the ice never melts,
I believe I will find you,
a small girl, frozen for ever in supplication.
I will take you in my arms,
and pray for your sweet warm flesh, carry you
back to yourself.

*

My little tiger with centuries on your shoulder,
you are eating me up.
Come out of the dark stripe of jungle
so I can see you.
Forget the savage river that sometimes is
and sometimes is not
and curl yourself around me as if only I am home.
Let me stroke your beautiful head.

*

I remember you in the gap between seconds,
in the time beneath time,
in the future that was not, in the dream of I am.

*

Soon there will be no possibility of this child
that I have named in absence: Jack,
for fathers and grandfathers.
Already he is fading, like an old family photograph,
ghosts in his eyes.

Snakeskin stilettos

Eight years old, you understand
these shoes are different.
Not for nothing
has your mother wrapped them in paper,
shut them into their box, set them
at the very back of the wardrobe.
Forbidden.

You imagine them –
on their own in the dark,
hissing softly.
Biding their time.

Sneak in, creak open the door,
lift the lid and let them out,
untissue the fear.
Run your fingers
Against the fissley scales,
press the fangs of heels
into your palm.
Something
you've never felt before.
These shoes are live and dangerous.

My turn to be the horse

I paw the tarmac,
snort long plumes of breath,
rejoicing in the strength
that flows along my back.
Muscle on bone
my strong straight limbs.
Sound joyful, rolls from belly
to trumpet-nostrils, trembling air.
Then rider taps a signal – go – and I

am
  rhythm
      running
           no walls stop

leap
  higher
      wider
          into air

hooves
  crack earth
        spark stars
              blood gallops

loose. The bell rings, calling us again
to be corralled, and we trot into line.
Horse and rider tamed by long division,
comprehension, back to little girls.
Under the desk my hooves dissolve.

Changes

In mad March, nights with a blood moon,
I slip into the skin of a hare,
to run the fields, leap at the sky –
out from the pressed earth that holds my form.

When opiate summer drugs the nights,
my skin is a snake's, coiled
around the cool centre of knowing.
I hold serpent secrets, my eyes are planets.

I am never afraid in the thick hide of bear,
dipping my paws in icy rivers
to scoop and eat silver-quick swimming life.
All winter my belly is full, my sleep deep.

Leda

All night she dreamt swan.
Warm rush of wings, cool beak on skin.
It did not occur to her to wonder
as she rose in a coupling of flight to bone,
throat on soft throat, speaking
the language of birds.

Only in the morning,
brushing down from her hair,
did she consider the event strange.

Raven

I foresee this moment:
I am lifted out of the Ark's dark belly, into the light.
Released from the tight cup of her hands, flight fills me again.
I will owe nothing.

Dream after Newgrange

I

Needing a break,
they took a long weekend,
caught the sun
on a beach in the south.
The first real warmth
in a cold late spring,
winds from the north.
It lifted them,
gave them back appetite,
so that they slept close,
woke early to the singing of birds.
Driving home again
they stopped at Newgrange,
bought ice cream
and joined a queue to see inside.

Plunged into darkness
at the stone centre,
she reached for his hand,
held it tight,
but had no sense of him,
or of herself.
Lost in the absolute
absence of light.

II

At dawn her flesh sings
under his palm.
She is a bird, dreaming
in deep green forests

where mysteries need no solutions.
Light is a fine precious beam
and she is feathered with praise.

Lust

Bearded old satyr,
the wind from the hills
is thick with your scent,
musty yet fresh,
a confusion of seasons.

Comfortable in the house of Pentheus,
with its fitted concepts,
its rational doors, leading always
from one place to the next,
she forgot you – became only human.

Then you rear again at her window,
swirled in your own myth.
Lines from an ancient script
calling her out into the hills,
where coiled snakes will lick her face
in the back seat of a parked car.

Vampiress

No mortal dreams remain.
Thirst wakens me
to a narrow darkness,
night-black against
my sin-white skin.
The scent of your blood
is musk – like love.
My appetite is infinitely keen.

Come to the window,
let me in. I am your own
come back for you.
Don't be afraid my sweet,
to feel my sharp little teeth
against your skin.

Poem found in a castle

Summer, when the hounds skulk
in buttress shadows, their tongues lolling,
this room remains damp, chill.
Its stone holds twelve months' winter,
and forty winters have folded over me
in this ancestral place, where faith
is rock on rock, piled to the sky.
My husband led me to this chamber,
and I was cold despite the fire's burning.
He placed a torc of silver on my neck,
called me his wife; but I dreamt of my sisters,
woke as ice, in stone-grey castle air.

From the window I see my dark-haired sons
ride out with their father to hunt wild things.
They don't look back, but know I stand here
framed in stone: their cold and foreign mother.
I dream I am the falcon on his wrist; hooded,
I see no place to land, but back to him.

The Irish dervish

After the poteen had been passed round,
Tona – beatified – closed his eyes,
bare-knuckled the beat until blood flew
from his fingers: anointing us.
Hammered by live bones, the bodhrán's skin
sang raw and red: thrilling, speeding
settled rhythms of heart and mind.
Spirits possessed us, held us
to a strange bliss, while the room
spun – faster and faster –
about the centre where he stood.

Snow White

One bite
and it was as if I were dead.
You anointed me, dressed me in finery
and laid me in my crystal box.
You placed beside me the few artefacts of my life,
then closed the lid and, weeping all the while,
shouldered my small weight to a clearing in the forest.
You left me there.
All this was done according to tradition.
Left to myself,
deer grazed at my feet, and on winter nights
the moon shone full in my face.
I saw seasons as ebb and flow of light
and knew myself as many things,
a vixen's footprint in new snow,
the delicate breastbone of a dove,
a stone held in a child's hand,
the apple in my own throat,
the kiss . . .

Easter cottage

Following a hand-drawn map
they find their next week's home
in turf-sweet darkness,
four miles outside the village.
A place in nowhere,
a bubble in time,
someone else's life
they walk into, instantly
make their own.
Stones from the beach,
shells, a bird's skull, it is
as if they'd gathered them
themselves on winter walks.
Shelves of books
they'd always meant to read.
Comfortable in the deep dark,
they love in Braille,
sleep as sound as the bodies
under the bog: their otherselves.

A temporary lease

I

Under Binevenagh and Eagle Hill,
in the Umbra, a thick green magic
veins the rock, runs through sap.

II

Across the railway tracks,
down a dark tunnel,
branches and brambles,
the hidden rambling house.
Sun-spotted, through leaves
of oak and beech.
Grown from one stone room,
earth-floored, dark:

to a flowering of pantries,
bedrooms and bathrooms.
Then all the rest –
as each new generation
felt a need for more.
The last a ballroom,
parquet-floored and huge,
French windows opening to air.

III

Tenanted there,
we dreamt a year –
tree-green days

of talk and music.
Grass-smoke nights
when we were satisfied.

Time changed to liquid,
so that we drifted between centuries,
traversed lifetimes.
Back and forth so easily,
we learnt to hear ghosts,
lived with their conversations.
Rhythms of dancing feet,
echoes of love in an empty room.

Each time we ventured out,
the world was always further.

In that year we loved forever.

After the argument . . .

we offer each other little treats.
Touch often, but with gentleness,
as if our skins might bruise
beneath the most delicate of caresses.
I bring flowers back into the house.
Vases full of heady honeysuckle,
minty hyssop. You cook omelettes
with brown eggs warm from straw;
we eat from the same plate.
Solicitous, we're careful in what we say,
for having thought ourselves immune
to chills, jealous fevers – it's shaken us.
We go to bed early on clean fresh sheets,
swear to take more care of ourselves.

Flirtation

The sky is restless, sensual,
charged with a promise of thunder,

and he sparks with you, first glance.
He's witty, charming, funny,

live with the static of desire.
No touch entirely accidental,

and his words, rising into the dark
like fireflies, possibilities.

He meets your eyes, raises his glass
in an unspoken promise – passion,

new territories mapped on skin in truth –
but you hear the lie in it. Outside

the sky breaks to rain, and you take
a taxi home to a warm domestic bed.

Infidelities

After he'd gone,
she found money in the sheets,
fallen when he pulled his trousers off.
Gathering the coins into a small pile,
she set them on the window ledge.
They sat, gathering dust, guilt,
until one day her husband
scooped them into his pocket.
Small change for a call
he couldn't make from the house.

Poisoned glen

Hold your breath.
A woman could drown
in these dark loughs,
cold as forever.
Learn how to stop
at the surface,
see no deeper.
It is a kind of courage
to hear only what is said
  I love you
balanced on liquid tension
like a pond skater.

Beneath, something almost seen,
a fin's flash in the dark weeds.

Kissing ghosts

I'm as dark as the sky, tired as the year,
and it's a wet, cold night: miserable.
All I really want is my seat by the fire,
TV turned on, mind turned off.
Instead I'm driving into town –

at the red light, my windscreen
blurs and clears
with the metronome of wipers,
so that every other second I see them.
Half inside a doorway,
half out in the rain,
kissing as if there were no weather.
He slips his hand inside her coat.
She tilts her hips towards him,
hand on the small of his back,
pulling him closer.
Their eyes closed,
their mouths urgent.

In the crowded bar, a man
takes the seat beside me.
Fortyish and balding,
he sits down heavily,
stares at me.
'Moyra,' he says at last,
'it is, isn't it?' I'm suspicious:
I don't know this man,
his heavy Doric voice.
'Dave,' he persists.
'Don't you remember
the scooter ride we took?'
And from nowhere I do remember –

see him again:
a Scottish boy on a red Vespa.
He calls at my door, and I
hold him tight around the waist
as we take to the road together.

I search for a trace
of that boy I kissed
in the face of this intrusive stranger,
middle-aged and overweight.
He gives me a résumé
of his life to date.
His time in Stirling, his book,
the failed marriage,
a son he never sees.
He pauses, waits for me to speak,
and I oblige, reduce down
twenty years to five or six
brief sentences.

A silence grows;
he buys me a drink
and, leaving, bends close
to touch his lips against my cheek.

Driving back alone from Mayo

No need for signposts
in a country crisscrossed
with trails of other journeys,
winter sun at my back
pushing me east.
I bless each familiar thing
and set my mind on constancy,
telling myself stories we could become,
reinventing our history.
I was faithful, content;
love made you articulate.
The fiction of what should have been
is a map unfolding, a way home.

Students in Athens

In a cool square, out of the main city swelter,
beneath the shade of an olive tree,
a young man leans back in his chair.
He drains his cup of thick black coffee,
then lights a cigarette. He is content as a cat.
The young woman with him raises a camera.

A year from now, when they are no longer lovers,
she will think of that momentary eternity,
the leaves of the olive dripping shadows
across the white tablecloth, the secret knowledge
of her body, touched only by him and the sun.
Bitter and sweet.

Twenty years from now, she'll come across
the photograph at the back of a drawer
and be taken aback at how young they were.
She'll feel a restlessness and wonder
whatever became of them.

Trabane

I weave this summer's time
on memory's frame.
Weft of air, warp of water
catching all the light.
Azure meeting of sky and lake,
red pools of sun's sinking.
I hold every colour, lichened boulders,
sea shades and coral strands,
where children touched with gold
climb rocks for starfish, shrimps.
Among the purple-brown Twelve Bens
I weave our love's calm colours
through passion's bright threads –
sleep beautiful. Winter
I'll throw this cloth across our bed.

The last summer

The dulse they picked is drying in the sun,
white with sea salt, sharp to taste.
Little flat fish wriggle beneath her toes.
Daddy holds her hand against the waves,
while mummy watches from a deckchair
on the sand. Faces smiling: her family.
Then quietly, nights closed in,
and autumn returned them home.

Pots they stacked, neat in rows,
grass mowings, language beneath.
In long shadow, behind the hedge,
her uncle gardens betrayal, an adult pain.
She becomes an initiate in silence.
As grown-up secrets seed,
daddy lets go of her hand,
mummy doesn't see her any more,
and she learns how to pretend,
becomes one of the family.

The shutter closes, takes and holds.
Always their faces; always the pose.

Catching the Liverpool boat

for S

You were the girl!
Free from family
and small-town eyes,
you hit the city.
Parties and pints
in the Club Bar,
where you could pull
any man you wanted –
and why not?
Sauce for the gander,
and all that.
Many's the one
was set on fire
by the bright flame
of your hair.

No big deal,
you said,
but when you came back,
you scissored your hair
to a pool on the floor,
swirling about your feet
bright as fresh blood.

She dreams . . .

The young man is peeling her an orange
while a foreign sun ripens outside the window.
His fingers, juicy, separate each segment carefully.
She is calm, knowing he will simply place the fruit
on a white plate and offer it to her.
She is not his wife or mother,
or anything she doesn't know how to be.
He is not her lover, though she knows
how his skin would taste.
The orange is sweet, the room is quiet.
No one speaks her name.

The young man has made her a poem
by erasing words, lines, even whole stanzas.
As he hands her the page, clean and white,
the final metaphor flutters to the floor.
She has no fear, knowing he will leave it unsaid:
there is no question, no rhyme or reasoning.
Even his eyes say nothing.

Hearts

All day he works with hearts,
to understand them better,
know how this muscle pumps,
contracts to its function.
In his palm the rabbit's heart
still flutters, as he injects
the enzymes, breaks it down.

Brought to its single self
under the microscope, each cell
reveals to him its nature,
gives measured answers.
Chromatographic shades of meaning
extracted, written down, definitive.

At night, he lays his head
on the soft billow of her breast,
hears the measuring of time, and all
heart's anarchies beat in his ear.

The apothecary

for John

He understands the garden, works
with its seasons. Nothing lies fallow.
Hedges protect, shelter new green.
Sap runs to the core, brilliant,
so the earth does not smell of decay.
He has planted herbs for healing;
nothing grows in vain. Even names
become a litany against dis-ease,
sweet and musical upon her tongue.
Comfrey, feverfew, valerian,
Amara dulcis, angelica, golden thyme.
Seeds of peony in wine to cure the nightmare;
oil of cowslip to assuage the forgetful evil.
By old remedies and the art of ordinary means,
patiently, he conducts her to health.
Blue stars of borage to gladden her heart;
eyebright, so she can see the colours of his love.
He has made an apothecary's den,
where bees drink from honeyed cups
and small birds tumble branch to branch.
Distillations of scent and sound
lift on the morning air to her bedroom window:
dreams of lushness; fragrant awakening.

Claire and the moon

Tonight the moon hung low, full,
bloated with summer.
Feeling its pull we went outside,
where silver half-light
showed the familiar strange.
Pipistrelles swooped to feed, calling.
I was too old to hear them
but they spoke for you.
Fat hens shuffled on their perches,
uneasy, as across the field
a dog fox looked for shadow.

Suddenly, letting go of my hand,
you raised your arms to the sky
and danced: a small dance
there on the shining grass –
your partner the moon, no part for me.

Kobi

A found poem

We were making the final preparations
for the New Year Tea Ceremony
when the earth leapt up with a sound like doom.
We have a saying:
if a thing happens twice, it will happen again.

Make hay

Summer fades from skin
and the pull begins, down.
Limbs grow heavy, light leaves
through the top of my head.

Outside, colours grow colder.

I find myself loitering outside florists
among buckets of bright flowers,
jittery as a user who needs to score.
On my back, the monkey of winter.

from *Beneath the Ice*

(2001)

The night of my conception

Rosalyn Avenue is quiet, darkness
laps at the small pool of light
spilling from the window of my parents' house:
their first home together. Today
they have painted the bathroom,
and a smell of paint lingers in the air.
My mother is in bed. Her stockings
drape the bedside chair and her hair is longer
than I remember it. She is listening
to the already routine sounds my father makes
as he shooshes the dog into the kitchen,
locks up for the night. His step
is quick and light along the hall,
as if everything is within reach.

He undresses, slips beneath the candlewick bedspread,
then lays his arm along the curve of her hip,
his hand warm and wanting
against the cool white sheen of her skin,
and she turns to him, needing love.

When he cries out his pleasure
she opens her eyes,
calls me by name –
and I am conceived inside her longing.
I will grow into the space between them.

Driving home from Saintfield

In memory it is always raining as we are leaving.
I wave goodbye to cousins, uncle, aunt:
always past my bedtime late.

Rain knuckles the roof,
but I am snug, safe in the car's cocoon,
the blackness held outside.

The wiper's jerk and thud, the heater's blast,
curves of country roads
carrying me to the soft verge of sleep

as we move homewards
along beams of light.
My mother is singing,

the 23rd Psalm; 'The Mountains of Mourne';
Clementine – *Oh my darling,*
oh my darling – just for me.

Lethe

My poor mother,
for your birthday you get another 'little episode',
another transient ischaemic attack,
during which you walk into a door jamb.
Your face is bruised, as if you'd been punched
hard, and when I ask if it hurts, you say
'I don't think so'. You are even more lost.
If only misery could be wiped away like memory,
like chalk-marks from a board, lessons over.

My poor mother,
your bones are light as the memory of bones,
and your flesh is melted to a dream of flesh.
My heart is broken by your lightness,
by your terrible absence, as you rest
what is left against my shoulder.
I cannot help you; there is no comfort,
and this is too cruel,
no matter what our sins have been.

My poor mother,
your children are unable, for even now
your need is not greater than ours,
and we have never known how.
Forgive us our trespasses
as we have forgiven your trespasses
against us. Deliver us
from this evil. Where is the river,
the beautiful, the beautiful, the river?

Daffodils

The Vertues: The roots stamped with hony, helpeth them that are burned with fire. They have also such wonderful qualities in drying, that they consound and glew together very great wounds.

Gerard's Herbal

I

I thought it was a fool's errand, thought
we'd never find the place,
my mother trying to navigate
with only a vague address to go by –
a farm somewhere outside Millisle.
My children bored, fighting in the back seat,
my nerves on edge, my hands too tight
on the steering wheel, stress levels high.

But we got there, loaded sackfuls of bulbs
into the car's boot, and paid the man.

For weeks afterwards, I'd look out the window
and see my mother on her knees, digging,
planting daffodils behind hedges, among trees.

II

My mother has descended into hell
(these biblical allusions haunt me),
and daffodils are the only colour in this Easter,
yellow incongruities across the dull fields,
painfully there, like the resurrection of love.

I cut them against despair, bring
huge bundles of them into the house,
beacons burning in vases, on windowsills.

Planter

My brother is a lean white shadow in the early-morning
  light,
unspoken things
have kept him thin, despite his wife's attempts to fatten him
  on love.

From the window I watch him walk his fields to their
  furthest edges,
where the deer graze.
He has dug himself a place, refused to be the seed on stony
  ground

and with a farmer's faith, he harvests himself against
  winter,
each winnowing
yielding the new history that he is planting in his children's
  hearts.

Words from the other side

I visited my friend in hospital
the day after she had died
and been brought back.
Her heart had stopped, exhausted
by another asthma attack,
by years of pumping
for an easy breath –
kicked back to life only
by doctors and electricity.

The air around her crackled.

Urgently
she pulled me close,
kissed my lips, placed
into the cave of my mouth,
onto my tongue,
a message for me, carried back –

'Death's easy,' she said,
'much easier than life' –

and her words hit me
like an amphetamine rush,
dizzied me, left me
electrified, unsure
if I'd been given
a blessing or a curse.

Outside

A window looks out onto a garden
where lupins, lilies and lobelias
turn the air heady, and butterflies
dip their long tongues into sweetness.

Almost hidden by profusion,
a gate opens onto a lane.

The lane wanders through hedgerows,
succulent and dripping
with honeysuckle and unpicked berries,
until it disappears over a hill
and out of sight
into some other vista.

A woman stands at the window,
and I imagine that she is watching
for someone, her child perhaps,
who will at any moment now
crest the hill, come into view.

When the child reaches the gate,
she will go through it,
cross the grass, enter the house
and open the door to the room
where the woman stands, waiting – except,
when I move closer to the window,
shading my sight from the sun's glare
on the glass, I see only my reflection.

There is no homecoming,
only my imagining, and perhaps
I have imagined the garden also,
the gate, the lane – even the window
where no one stands watching.

Poetry

I am being followed by a flock of winged words,
plagued by their black eyes and beaks.
Their tongues are sparks in the blue air
and I have heard their songs so often that I almost
understand the sense beneath the notes.
They make intricate iambic patterns round my head,
a lyric latticework, a tilt of time.
At night they roost along the window ledge,
and though I've nailed my window closed,
my last waking thought is always looking for its rhyme.

Three ring

When I am born,
my family sit my plump little feet
onto the wire, so that I know its feel.
When I am four, I can walk its length
with hardly a wobble. I'm in the Big Top
at seven, performing without a net,
my dress hand sequinned, my hair curled.
By ten I'm famous, known
to circus lovers everywhere.
They adore my exquisite balance,
gasping with pleasure
as I leap and pirouette
to always land steady,
my body absorbing the wire's jangle.
It is my special talent
to never think about falling.

When I'm fifteen
I marry the lion-tamer's son.
He strokes me as if I am
dangerous, enters me trembling
while the great beasts
lean against the bars, throats purring.

Gravity comes into my limbs
and falling into my heart.

The visitor

A December evening.
a minute before midnight,
and a bird begins to sing
from a branch in the ash tree
just outside our bedroom window.
It sings on through the night
until daybreak, its solitary trill
filling the air with sound, exotic,
notes rising and falling against the dark.

At first we are intrigued, delighted.
A nightingale? A nightjar?
No ornithologists, we wonder
if it is some bird that's lost its way,
blown off migratory course
by winter storms, to end up
singing at a time like this.

Then, as night after night it returns
to sing because it must,
to call a mate who never answers,
the novelty wears off.

Birdsong disturbs our sleep, our dreams
are filled with feathered longing as if
we too are being called by some thing
or some place we'll never reach now.

Lullaby

Tonight the air is thick with babies,
naked and mewing in the dark,
their blind fish mouths seeking.
They float unanchored, loose in time,
ebbing and flowing with my breath
as if I am the tide of the ocean.

There is no point
in asking why they're here. They're only
babies after all, wouldn't know
what I was talking about – so
I'll just gather shoals of them
in the nets of a remembered rhythm,
and sing myself, and them, to sleep.

Lately

I've come to dread dreams, phone calls,
visitors, messages from life's borders,
for these days
it seems all the news is bad,
and though I'm scrupulous
about such assurances
as saluting magpies, throwing salt
and touching wood, it is impossible
to feel safe or immune.

I am haunted by the ghosts of old men,
and I see how time runs
past old women, how they are left
stumbling after, gasping for meaning.
Even the children are touched by fear,
become harder to comfort.

Days are so out of kilter
that I catch glimpses of the future,
but always too late to stop what happens next.

Piano lesson

It must have been
the sound of the piano ghost
(downstairs all alone and weeping
little silvery notes) that started me

dreaming of the woman in the bath,
letting her wrists open to the warmth,
her blood flowering in the water
like the fronds of a sea anemone.

Anecdotal words

I

She works night shift, security, watching
the monitors, walls of glass, fragments
of city streets, moments of lives.
She sees all kinds of things pass by, tight knots
of drama, quick fucks in doorways, fights, tears
in the rain, drunks pissing against the wind.
Sometimes she dreams up histories, allows
these anecdotal thoughts to swell, become
stories for strangers moving through the dark –
like these two, faces lost in static snow.
Bereft of meaning or context, she gives
them hopelessness, illicit love, and ice,
a monster trapped inside a glacier,
a virus underneath the permafrost.

II

A Belfast Sunday is no place for late-night might-be lovers:
cold streets and closed doors, nowhere to go.
A security camera records their uncertainty,
him and her in a black-and-white loop, a B-movie,
grainy from re-running. She's shivering
and he leans against a stone façade, holds her
as the winter wind winds her coat around them.

He's offering anecdotal evidence of warmth,
and though his words have rhythm and scansion,
she knows they prove nothing: he will always be
nine-tenths hidden. Her words are a frozen weir
where a woman floats, dreaming beneath the ice.
His kisses will not warm her, nothing will melt;
there will never be anything between them but regret.

Applying fuzzy logic

To find your own niche in love's conceptual anarchy
forget Aristotle and his either/or logic –
go for fuzzification instead: the cocaine of science.

Enter your lover's linguistic variables, his if-then rules,
his vagueness, paradoxes and information granulation
into the Kosko Fuzzy Approximation Theorem.
Make use of the machinery

for dealing with imprecision and partial truth.
The outcome will define where love stands for you
on the continuum between completely true and completely false.

This allows you a closer rapport with reality,
and can substantially increase your power.

Out damned teeth marks

next morning she finds
the distinct marks of his teeth
on the palm of her hand
beneath her thumb a small bright bruise

and while she can shower
his touch from her skin
his smell from her fingers
this stigmata stays tender

a reminder
that something dangerous
has slipped its harness
but they are both sensible people really

and some days later
their sensible conversation
will use cliche
to rope it down again

drunk at the time
let's just pretend it didn't happen
then all she will have to do is wait
for the evidence to fade be gone

the theory's fine the difficulty is
that she is slow to mend
weeks later
a ghost trace still remains

her life's moved out of joint
as if the fates have turned
and she's begun to feel
like Lady Macbeth – indelibly stained

Bitten

She's not at all well –
sleeplessness
obsessive thoughts
lack of concentration
strange aches, dreams and cravings

Working on the principle of homeopathy and hangovers –
treat like with like/hair of the dog –
she pours herself a drink
and wonders if he'd agree
to be prescribed for her cure,
man as medicine, labelled
take as required
until the symptoms have resolved themselves.

The straw

she forgave him his trespasses,
those she knew, and those she guessed at,
so she would have found a way to forgive him
the dark-haired nurse with the coke habit –
same as the others – had it not been
for the day she came home from work
to find them both, smug
with post-coital repleteness
and just-dressedness on her new sofa
that she hadn't even got sitting down on yet herself

She's trouble

Saturday night,
after a few drinks,
he looks straight into her eyes,
takes her hand in his, says
she has no idea how good it feels,
asks if she doesn't love him just a little,
tempting her into compoundment
so that she goes and comes with him
so easily that she thinks maybe
she does love him – just a little.

Sunday morning,
after several cups of black coffee,
he looks sideways,
says it doesn't feel right, besides,
he'd had too much to drink, and drink
always gets him into trouble.

Small deaths

As all the years' growth engulfs my house,
branches block every view of further afield,
days dawn green and dense,
light ripples like water.
My breathing slows.

Outside the window,
behind my eyes,
everything is leaf and bird
and I grow accustomed
to the habits of sparrows,
thrushes, blackbirds, finches, starlings –
their songs a thread of accidental pleasure
that skeins my heart.
Best of all I love the wrens –
but their fragility frightens me
even though I understand
a dead bird is nothing.
You could barely weigh it in your hands.

The art of tying flies

He's tying a Red Sedge
for those hot summer evenings
or those dead afternoons, July and August,
when he can't quite decide
what to offer the occasional riser,
close under the bank.

The body is hare's ear, spun on orange silk,
and ribbed with gold wire.
Wound all down the body from head to tail,
the hackle comes from a red cockerel.
The wings are Landrail, tied so as to lie
flat along the Sedge's back.
Beeswax the thread, wind and tie,
interweave fur and feather
until they become a living creature again,
re-formed, reborn. Finished,
he holds it between his fingers,
lifts it into the light,
sees the graceful wheel of the line
as he lays it down soft as a snowflake

beautiful as any red sedge
fluttering late in the evening sun
on a slow-moving stream.

I am

I

Today I have been a comma
between
two halves of a story.
A salmon exhausted
against the flow.

Yesterday I was silk,
I was a sweet inhalation.
I was the wood's grain.

Tonight I am the oldest woman in existence
and I have a great sorrow, a divine sorrow
that covers the face of the earth with tears.
No ark will float on it nor rainbow arch it.

Tomorrow I will be a running hare.

II

I am serotonin, adrenalin,
hippocampus, synapse, nerve,
progesterone and oestrogen,
meat and juice, bone and dust.

Hurt

Stay perfectly still.
Time will take this past you
if you wait. Don't struggle.

Damaged moments
flapping and circling
like great clawed birds.

Flayed hours that rattle
like gales, snow laden
from the Arctic of your heart.

The questions you can't ask,
the answers you can't give,
the more you can't take –

sit it out – the nausea will pass.
Days will become linear again
and you'll resume the forward march.

Blue

Lying in the vicious dark
I close my eyes and bring back blue –
holiest, calmest of colours.

I send it round my veins, flood
the empty chambers of my heart with it,
douse myself in it.

I soothe the anxious air with it,
fill my children's rooms with it,
wrap them in soft swathes of it, safe

and I can sleep
rocked in a hammock of blue
sky above, sea below.

1st of the first

The old year
laid down into memory
like the ring of a tree, marking
another full circle completed

and the calendar's clean days
stretching forwards
untainted,
tempt me to hope.

I am resolved
to stub out past failures,
weigh myself
on tomorrow's scales.

Notice of eviction

You are hereby given notice
that from this day forward
your tenure has ceased.
You are therefore banned
from setting foot
in any thought process
(conscious or unconscious)
that belongs to me.

Under subsection C
this includes dreams and fantasies
whether or a sexual nature or not.

Please note: I shall be changing the locks.

Finding comfort in fractals

I imagine
applying the Mandelbrot equation
to the chaos of my life,
inputting the data of disorder,
the total randomness of it all,
thoughts and actions, desires and fears,
that change from day to day,
hour to hour, minute to minute

and finding in the end
nothing is random.
Finding beneath everything
a pattern –
beautiful as a fern, a coastline,
or the dance of planets.

Ulster says no

Having grown up with so many given negatives
I am always and constitutionally inclined to say yes
yes let's have another drink
yes go on ahead
yes of course you can
yes I'll try that
yes why not
yes have some of mine
even when it might be more prudent to decline.

If I asked you to

would you set down your drink,
get up from your seat
and dance me, waltz me
across this chequered floor, unclamp me
from the crocodile jaws of tedium,
lift me, defy my gravity, whirl me
away from black and white
and shades of grey,
decompose me to all the colours,
balance me on your fingertips
a rainbow arc, promise me,
delight me with delicacy, undo me,
help me out of my head
into the honeycomb of flesh
until I am sticky with sweetness: fill me

Postcard from the island of lizards

I am salamander in the all-day sun
among almonds and pomegranates.
As mornings liquefy to afternoons

I grow sweet and satisfied,
soaking light, warming bones.
A great turtle holds up the earth,

little salty fish leap to my dish
and thirst is a cool spring.
Nights I sleep in a white house

where Mary Mother of God
gazes on me with love. P.S.
dreams have returned.

Words from the past

A man from far away
has brought a gift you must accept
for he has crossed all the world's borders,
travelled through places you can only imagine,
to bring it to you, icy tundra in his eyes,
the wind howling your name.

You must invite him in,
take what he gives,
no matter what it is,
a white lily or a millstone,
a letter fallen from the pages of a book
you lift at random from the shelf.
A book you have not read for years,
communication from a previous life.

The prodigal daughter

That woman – the one who left the house
to buy a pint of milk, and then just disappeared –
has been found again, living on a beach,
identified. Despite the pleas
of family and friends, she declines
all offers of a ticket home and will not tell
the four-year story of her anonymity.

She shuns the fifteen-minute bribes
of newspapers and magazines,
preferring to remain balanced on her toes,
a ballerina on a jewellery box,
the mirror sea beneath.

She keeps her words there;
recites them to the holy blue of sky
and hears them back on tongues of birds,
sees their little tongues flicker
beneath the eggshells,
birthing an oratorio of wings.

Geography

I dream of maps
laid out across my table,
across my years, with little flags to mark
where such and such a thing happened,
pinpointing
which road was taken,
when and where the choice was made that led
to this particular configuration
of hills and valleys, the topography of now.

from *The Horse's Nest*
(2006)

Stubbs at Horkstow

Lord Nelthrope's boy
brings this one to me, not
the usual type, old and broken
but a handsome bay gelding,
still muscled up and fit,
crippled though, tendon
snapped on the hunting field,
no use to his Lordship now,
so kindly donated.

I hold the halter rope,
my assistant cuts the throat,
his knife well practised,
and the keen arc of jugular
blood marking the air
with its hot ferrous smell.
The boy cannot watch, pales,
has to be sent indoors
for a drink of water.

The horse goes down neatly,
onto his knees, onto his side,
feet jerking, mixing the mud
and blood into a red paste,
impasto-thick: we wait
until he stills and his eyes film,
then the rush to inject veins
and vessels with liquefied tallow
before they collapse.

The tackle is my own design,
an iron bar suspended
by a teagle to which iron hooks
are fixed. Pass these hooks
through the ribs, under the back-
bone, fasten them: so the corpse
is lifted, hung, hooves resting
on a plank, and I can set them
in the attitude of a horse walking.

It is a long journey
into the body of a horse,
into the structure of reality:
abdomen, five layers
of muscle, peritoneum,
pleura, lungs and bowels,
then the head, stripping
the skin until the muscles
are cleaned and ready
for me to make careful
diagrams, write detailed
explanations, the work
of a day and then another,
on and on, working against
time, the fattening flies,
the smell: I do not flinch.

Tollymore

My mother is no ghost
no presence no sign
nowhere

except
beside the Shimna,
where coming back is a counterbalance

to loss – the same paths walked
by generations, the same trees
shading

the paths
although the people
have gone into the flow of time.

June sun illuminates brackish water –
ripples over stone, shadow fish
flicking

their tails against the current.

*

The August forest smells different,
sweeter, decaying towards autumn.
Through the floor's moss and mulch,
fly agarics, yellow fingers of coral fungus.

We know these paths, and the difference:
rowan berries, blackberries, hazelnuts,
chestnuts, all ripening, and underneath,
the six swallowed pomegranate seeds.

*

The tail of Hurricane Charley
flicks us two days
and nights of wind and rain,
heavy, incessant rain.
We play cards, drink coffee
and lie awake, listening
to the downpour,

and the Shimna river,
beneath and above the rain,
a great liquid train
of memory,
roaring and rumbling
over rocks, down waterfalls
and out to sea.
We rescue what we can.

Monumental sculptor

When he has cut my mother's name
into the granite, McCormick,
the monumental sculptor,
ESTABLISHED SINCE 1938,
along with the invoice
sends photographs – proof.

The hummingbird case

I

Strung-up bones of the blue whale,
crystals and fossils and earthquakes;
the hummingbird case, hundreds
of dead hummingbirds, pinned
in attitudes of song and movement,
beaks open, wings outstretched,
fastened forever to a dead tree
in a glass cabinet, turned
wooden legs, decorative carvings
framing their limbo.
I can't take my eyes off it.

*

Bird of superlatives,
smallest warm-blooded creature,
the fastest metabolism,
smallest nest, fastest heartbeat,
fewest feathers of any bird,
best memory of any bird,
remembering how many flowers,
when each was last drunk from.

Bird who can fly right, left,
up and down,
upside down and backwards,
tips of the primary wing feathers
describing a perfect figure of eight
in axial rotation, wings beating
up to seventy times in every second.

The hummingbird, alone among the birds,
can hover
in perfectly still air.

*

Whitehead and Keates
are the museum's reference,
but they don't know much,
just that the cabinet is walnut
and oak, early nineteenth century
probably, probably listed
in the sale catalogue
for Mr Bullock's Egyptian
Hall, Piccadilly.

A good example,
made purely
as a conversation piece.
A pseudo-natural prop
(in this case a tree) to set off
the greatest number of objects,
here, around five hundred birds,
a guess from the tour guide
who tried to make the count.
The world's smallest bird,
the bee hummer,
is trapped here too.

*

Bird from the Left, the spirit land,
messenger between worlds
who knows the secret doors
and passageways: bringer
of smoke to the shaman, tongue

piercer, rain maker, glittering
rainbow fragment, earrings
for Aztec priests, your feathers, held
up to the sunrise at winter solstice,
hasten the rebirth of the stillborn.

II

The parlour maid is a flibberty-
gibbit, so the Colonel's wife
inspects the room herself,
runs her fingers along
the mantelpiece for dust,
adjusts the stems of calla lilies.
A good fire, the silver polished,
candles lit and multiplying
in facets of crystal; the Colonel
needs everything to be perfect.
A year they've been married,
time enough for her to learn
how important it is
to keep the Colonel happy.

She lifts a spoon, and sees herself
distorted by the curve, her pale face,
the darkness beneath her eyes.
She pats her hair, run through
and through with hairpins
to keep its unruliness in check.
The Colonel won't have imperfection.
She sets the spoon down
on the pristine white
starched linen tablecloth.
Her nerves are bad today,
she hasn't felt right
since she first set

eyes on that horrible
bird cabinet he bought
last week in Piccadilly.
A real conversation piece
he said as the men carried
it in, set it beneath the tiger's
head and the elephant tusks.

Last night she dreamt the glass
was broken and the tiny creatures
loose, escaped around her head,
a blur of wings, ruby throats
and stabbing beaks.
She tried to shoosh them away,
flapping her hands, but they flew
into her hair, her eyes, her mouth.

III

THE EGYPTIAN HALL.

Roll up, roll up
to a CORNUCOPIA of wonders and marvels –

We have on display NAPOLEON'S CARRIAGE
taken at Waterloo: antique marbles, jasper, agate,

vases, tablets, tazzas, superb pictures
of the ANCIENT and MODERN Masters.

NATURAL CURIOSITIES: snakes and crocodiles,
a six-legged pig, an ELEPHANT, a RHINOCEROS,

many more strange and wonderful sights
from far-off lands and SAVAGE JUNGLES.

Our suggested tour begins with a case of artefacts
from the SANDWICH ISLANDS, many of them

brought back by the celebrated CAPTAIN COOK.
See the wonderful collections of exotic birds

from the AMERICAS and AMAZONIA.
The magnificent plumage of the Bird of Paradise,

tiny jewelled humming birds,
sought out and captured, BROUGHT TO YOU

by that other esteemed explorer of our age,
Mr HUMBOLDT.

Mr WILLIAM BULLOCK's amazing collection,
formed during seventeen years of arduous research

at a cost of thirty thousand pounds, is open to everyone –
ADMISSION ONLY ONE SHILLING.

IV

Yes, ours is a successful business –
taxidermy for the modern scientific age.
We supply the guns and traps and nets
and my son does the travelling, away
for months at a time, sea voyages, Mexico,
Tahiti, the Americas: where explorers go.

He has nimble fingers and he's good at his work:
the peeling and cutting must be done delicately,
not clumsily, or the skin may be torn. Taught him
myself: first the back cut from neck to tail, remove
the organs, all the viscera, tongue, trachea, taking
great care to scrape off all the fat, then rub the skin
with a mix of ash, sulphur and alum – that way
they get home to me safe and well preserved.
Lately he's been trying a new recipe, some
French gent's: arsenic in it. You're right,
I'm not one for change for change's sake,
but I'd have to say, the arsenic does a fine job.

I must confess, this last commission's
been a challenge, with my eyesight
not so good and such a number of birds,
hundreds and hundreds – and so tiny,
smaller than the wrens that nest the hedges
round our house, but brighter than wrens,
like little jewels; one small as an insect.
Fiddly to stretch such small scraps of skin
over the artificial bodies; awkward to stuff
with hay, fiddly to stitch: such small skewers
to fix them to the branch, positioning each
bird so that the whole display's in balance.

I think I've got it right, like if I clapped
my hands the lot would just take flight.

I bring an artist's eye to the natural world
even if I say so myself; in years to come,
people will look at this case of birds
and see it as a work of art as much as any
painting or sonnet or sonata, don't you think?
What else is art but the ability to capture life,
pin it down to be admired and wondered at.

V

I know myself
when out of the blue heaven
you plummet before me
a breathless piece of sky
so for a moment I believe
you are the sky
and your bird shape
just light's desire for physicality

you rise and fall with such mastery
how can I not open myself
red petal and nectar: flower for you.

VI

I am the hummingbird the Navajo sent up
to see
what is above the blue sky: that found nothing.

Something and nothing

. . . and I am re-begot
Of absence, darkness, death; things which are not.
John Donne, A Nocturnal upon S. Lucy's Day, being the
shortest day.

Wren
  on the windowsill,
            an omen   maybe,
      sends
                            my heart flying. I am nothing
if not easy to please:
    then
            the familiar fraction,
        yin of fear
at the heart of every confidence.
                    Today
our time is doubly stolen,
                        borrowed
        from an overdraft,
                    all
                    capital depleted:
yet for these hours,
      nothing
is everything,
            a remembered taste
fed mouth   to mouth,
rhythm
on
rhyme,
      like the building of grace,
            curving
and

I am   in danger,
     dissolving,   losing
the line,
          becoming
something   else.

Lightning strike

The calm afterwards holds
a mesmerising light.
We go outside,
into the discharged evening,
the palpable vibration of atoms;
down the shimmering lane,
to look for the glass dagger.

The gorse bush is charred
to its bare bones, the earth still
smoulders from the piercing.

Mist rises towards the moon
from the thick drenched grass
of the hayfield, where a black stag
antlered with silver is watching us.

Yourself

Do not give yourself up for a god.
Do not give yourself up for a master.
Do not give yourself up for a parent.
Do not give yourself up for a husband.
Do not give yourself up for a child.

Complaints

I

My lover is the wind,
inconstant, nothing
but change without substance,
hot and cold, whisper, roar,
and me the silly
spinning weather vane.

II

My lover is a natural disaster,
earthquake, famine,
a plague of locusts;
I am uninsurable.

III

My lover is a broken reed
and I have nothing to lean on.

Marriage poem

Secretive again, the evening drifts towards darkness,
the weight of nothing expected – a moth wing brush.
The white freesia, the bamboo blind, the gift horse;
moving between dimensions with the obstinate grace
given to familiar objects and their place in our lives.
What we ignore will never forgive us.

I have left you the torn map and the silence –
will you find me? Will you look in the twilight
where memories drop like bats from the eaves
of the house where we believed, where the garden
grew us and the children conceived us, before the wind
stormed through our hearts and the rains fell?
This is what I can and cannot say – longing never ends,
is the round smooth stone that I hold in my hand.

In the gallery of sleep

The dream is like a painting:
man on clifftop, the sea
raging beneath.
A fierce wind blowing,
as can be seen by the way
the man is leaning
and the way
the grass is flowing
round his feet.
Rain comes down
in oblique silver streaks.

The dreamer is like a woman
viewing the painting,
providing the narrative.
She is worried either
for the man or for herself,
she's not sure which.
She reaches up,
touches the glass,
which is all
that separates her
from the man and the storm.
You'll close
the window, crawl
back towards
sleep, back
through too much
time, mist that
sunlight cannot pierce.

A free lunch

Across the table from this man
who is buying her lunch
she finds herself thinking
of Red Riding Hood
and how the woodcutter
sliced open the wolf's belly
and filled it with stones.
She sees this man
who is buying her lunch
sinking into a river.
She sees his stone-loaded
belly dragging him down.
He looks surprised
as the last of his breath rises
through the water.
She likes this man
who is buying her lunch,
but still, something
about him has brought her
this image of violence,
drowning and stones.

A dangerous woman

i.m. Noelle Vial

Her hands in the washing-up bowl, sudsy and warm –
she's a woman who believes in love, miracles
in the kitchen, an angel to trouble the water,
a man to run his fingers across her belly, melding
the edges of where she's been sawn in two,

a woman who believes she can make
something truthful from the soft shape
of a child's throat, a raised fist, a bed
of nettles, a silk blouse; who believes
she can say anything given by air and angels,
by the way a line carves across a white page.

Tongue

I plant the wizened seed of my head
in the winter earth. My tongue stills,
curls back on itself like an old manuscript.
We sleep, the earth and me, all through
the darkest days and dreamless nights
until light begins again and my head
becomes white and tuberous, my green
daughters growing from my eyes,
my tongue a root, sucking nurture
from the death of what was; from
my third eye, a shoot: white flowers.

Tao

One magpie, sorrow
on the monkey puzzle tree,
preening its feathers.

Dark

The past comes towards me,
arms outstretched, needing
comforted like a small child
who has woken in the dark.

A local tragedy

Because I was a small child and impressionable
when my mother told me how they stood
at the door and watched the ambulances go past
I felt I'd been there too,
                                    saw the tense-faced men,
felt the lashing rain, the wind that would blow you
off your feet it was that strong. I heard the sirens
clanging from Ards past the farm at Drumhirk,
fading on through the Cotton and Ballyvester
to Donaghadee and the Imperial Hotel
where they brought the survivors
and the bodies, the day of the Great Storm,
the day the *Princess Victoria* sank in the waters
around Mew Island, within sight of shore.

  It happened years before I was born, the story's
  not mine at all: yet I come back to it as if it is.

There was nothing to suggest this crossing
would be different to any other, even with
a storm blowing up as the ship slipped her buoy.

They met the first big sea just past Cairnryan,
waves that smashed the steel doors of the car deck.
A catalogue then of fear and desperation,
mistakes, misinformation, the SOS in Morse
as the radio operator stayed at the transmitter,
the passengers in top-deck lounges
and smoking rooms where walls had become
floors when the ship listed onto her beam-ends.
Life jackets donned, rafts filled with the women
and children, splintered in the waves, lifeboats

launched from Donaghadee and Portpatrick:
while the sea took its course and the ship rolled over, sank.

This was the sea I paddled in, ankleted by tiny fish;
where wavelets sushed the shore and seaweed,
drawn aside, revealed a sideways scuttle of crabs.
Limpets and periwinkles in salty rock pools,
the bloom of sea anemones, harvest of dulce
all the teeming childhood summer – where now
in dreams I saw the drifting faces of the dead,
and heard across sleep the great tenor G
of Mew Island foghorn, sounding mortality.

The bodies washed ashore for days along
the Scottish coast, the Isle of Man, Port Luce, Hango
Hill, Kentraugh, Castletown and Arbory, one hundred
and twenty-eight drowned, thirty-three survivors.
Reports name only a few, Captain James Ferguson
who went down with his ship, the politicians, Major
Sinclair, Sir Walter Smiles; a handful of the crew.
The others, our 'fellow citizens', aren't singled out

but imagine just one, one woman, or man, or child,
as mouth and nose and lungs fill with the icy cold.

*

From my bathroom window, every seven seconds
I see the clear white strobe of Mew Island light.
It illuminates the land between me and the sea,
between me and the child I was

a landscape out of ordinary time,
where years slip and reshuffle,
the under-layers rising into white
light and dipping beneath again.

Small details and swathes of history:
who knows what will be thrown up
and what is mine?

In Francis Street my grandmother,
recently widowed,
opens her eyes to another day.
Her sister Maggie's there to help
and upstairs, wee Jack is snuggled up
in bed with his five brothers.

Betsy hitches her father's horse
to the block wheel cart to follow her lover,
sets off from the Six Road Ends to meet
death on a battlefield in Ballynahinch.

       Glaciers sweep across, gouging out the crag
                    and tail of Scrabo Hill.

       Vikings sail the lough, bury their battle dead
             on the beach at Ballyholme.

       Mrs McCoubrey's little ginger dog
       barks at me through a hole in the hedge
       as mummy calls me in for tea and bath
                    and bed.

     Comgall rises at five AM to pray,

   my daddy rises at five AM to go to work.

I watch the bones of history settle to dust
and rise again to walk, to speak –
make room for memory of us
our ordinary extraordinary lives
made up of moments just like this and this and this.

*

I have been told that his Morse code was immaculate until the very end
William Broadfoot

Radio Officer Number R 218736,
David Broadfoot, 53,
employee of the Marconi Wireless
Telegraph Company, calmly
amidst the chaos and the noise,
despite the angle of the listing ship,
the pitch and roll, signalled
so that others might live.

At 13.30 hours the order came –
abandon ship. At 13.58
the last message was received
. . . − − − . . .
At 14.00 hours she sank.

*

Of course the ship was not seaworthy:
an enquiry found the owners negligent
on at least two counts.

There are no accidents,
say the bones

and sometimes I hear them
all at once, asking
for remembrance.

*

On Boxing Day TV
I watch a woman run
not away but towards the wave,
towards a cliff of death,
towards her family.

Bangor girls, 1960s

Bangor girls are beautiful and bright and blessed
by tennis courts and ponies, mothers who drive them
to elocution classes and pick them up from parties:
fathers who bring them shoes from Carnaby Street.
The streets they stroll, arm in arm, are leafy – Farnham,
Knockmore, Seacliff – houses guarded by stone lions,
driveways and intricately wrought iron gates, behind
which the Bangor girls do homework, practise scales
and dream of futures bright and beautiful and blessed
as they: they wear their youth around them, as if
naiveté's a charm to keep all evil things at bay.
They will not fade, nor fail, nor falter: they believe.

Water

Water is not afraid,
it plunges over cliffs
and does not hesitate
to go into deep ravines
and places of filth.

In its humility
water always seeks
the lower ground
and so accumulates:
gathers strength
from its own fall.

Summer of entanglement

I

House spider

I hear her feet on the wooden floor,
then at first sight, think its a mouse,
or my own hallucinatory creature
moving in from the peripheral,
but it's house spider, grown
to monstrous dimensions in the heat
of our comfortable, insulated life.

I call for help and when help
captures her, she fills the whole
circumference of a pint glass
with her huge obscenity, natural,
unnatural: she glares through
the transparent curve between us,
fixing me, sizing me up.

II

Holiday house spiders

Dots with legs,
hanging,
ready to descend
on their steel ropes,
miniature paratroopers,
fast and brutal

catch and eat

then up again
to the bedroom ceiling.

If I can fall asleep
With them above me
I can cope with anything.

III

Crab spider ♀

Every time I rinse a cup,
or fill the kettle,
or simply glance out,
I see her, creamy white,
all abdomen and patience,
fattening on the insects
brought to her web by the light
from our kitchen window.

I am entangled:
her single-minded spinning,
the delicate angles,
the shape
of her life.

IV

Dream spider

I wake to find two
fang marks
and a trickle of blood
on my toe.

V

Crab spider ♂

He turns up late
when summer's
nearly over.
Smaller, darker,
quicker than her,
for several nights
he dashes concentric
approaches, jagged
with fear and pheromones
until eventually she has him.

VI

Crab spider ♀

She's gone, but all around the window's edge
are bulging pearly sacs of spider eggs.

VII

The spider Love

> . . . *we have bene begotten miraculously,*
> *fostered and geen sucke more straungely* . . .
> —from North's translation of Plutarch's *Life of Romulus*

Did you know that cobwebs used to be laid across wounds
to seal them, allow them to heal? Cobwebs against my skin.
They had wrapped me, swaddled me in silk. Bundled me up.
Safe. We lived mostly in the dark, mostly in silence, and I
was happy just to be there, unable to move or see. I felt
their touch on my face as they fed me, and I could have

stayed there forever if they had not begun to slowly unwrap me. I became aware of my body, its fleshiness, compared to their brittle delicacy. I hoped I could become the same as them. They comforted me with beauty, spun from their own bellies. Exquisite angles. They created the alphabet. Without them you would never have heard this story. They taught me to make patterns, and although I was slow and clumsy at first, they were never discouraging. They would bring me more silk. They taught me patience, how to sit and wait. They taught me quickness, how to strike. Living in the rhythm of dust my limbs began to desiccate, as if I was with gratitude becoming one of them.

Miss Mary Anning

It is certainly a wonderful instance of divine favour – that this poor ignorant girl should be so blessed . . .

Entry in the diary of Lady Harriet Silvester after
visiting Mary Anning in 1824

In my portrait I am staid
and fat and stiff, bonneted,
caped, carrying the tools
of my trade, hammer
and collecting bag,
little dog at my feet,
companion on expeditions
up and down the coast.

My father loved to tell
the story of my survival,
the travelling circus,
everyone flocking out
to see the dwarves,
the bearded lady,

then the lightning,
our neighbour falling,
blackened, to the ground,
smoke rising from her head
and me still cradled in her arms.

Father insisted that I
became much livelier
and smarter afterwards,
insisted I'd been marked
out. Some said I'd been
gifted a flash of God-
sight, a vision of an older

140

Dorset, under-layers,
ancient bones and shapes.

Nonsense. The leap
of imagination was mine
that solved the riddle
of the bones. Ichthyosaurus,
plesiosaur. The work
was mine, ten years
on each, delicately
uncovering, skilfully
reconstructing,

then my name ignored,
what I achieved put down
to the miraculous.

No one can foretell what
life will lay down, stratum
upon stratum, the bones
of self, geology of cancer.
If I am bitter,
could I be blamed,
even by my family's
stern, dissenting God?

In my portrait I am bland,
serene, contented,
bonneted, caped,
my little dog at my feet.

Girls and horses

Deconsecrated from the church of the economy,
horses are given over to us, droves of little girls.
We clamber the bone-littered killing fields
in mutual rescue, we suck it up, the heady smell
of horse, the horse that sees us when we need
nothing more than to be seen: in our hall
of mirrors he is a way out. We keep our secrets
when we leave the stable, our understanding
of dirt and strength and pain and sweat.
Delicate and powerful, feared and fearful,
girls and horses, one creature.

Notes towards a February poem

Pain is waiting in the nerves: the hawk is waiting on the wing.

I do not like this dream,
the house, the rooms where doors open only inwards
and everything is dusty, dark, neglected;
where I am lost.

What do you want from me, you whipped dog,
you small cur of grief sitting beside me, always pleading
and always there? Do not go on and on like this.

I have forgotten much more than I remember,
huge tracts of memory, like tundra, bare and featureless.

I am the girl with the beautiful horse, full of grace
in the split-second of suspension.

Harvest

Thinking back, the only strange thing
was her wearing her coat night and day,
even when it was warm.

We worked from dawn to dusk,
bringing in the winter bedding,
and I kept pace, hefted
the bales against my thigh,
passed them to my father
who was stacking: my hands
were blistered, shoulders sore.

My brother and my mother, back
and forth with the tractor and trailer
to the field, all of us lifting, sweating,
rain forecast, clouds gathering,
the job to be finished.

Later, when the pains tightened,
I left the exhausted house
and went back out to the barn.
I made a nest beneath the curved
tin roof and when he was born
I held him, little blue star,
then hid him again, rain on the roof
like the beating of starling wings.

January it was he found it
wedged between two bales
right at the back of the barn.
He laid it out on a bed of straw
then called me to see.

When we asked her, she told us all
but its father's name.
We buried it in the bog field;
that seemed the best thing to do.

Carp

Success never closes
its eyes, never
stops swimming.

The Phoenix Clinic

This is landscape
laid waste,
scorched and cratered,
ash-grey, unpeopled and silent.

Where would you look for hope
in such a landscape? And yet
these trees, stunted and twisted,
still reach their fingers skywards,
where one small thread of light comes through,

and I am reminded of the gingkos
less than a mile from ground zero in Hiroshima:
a few months later, budding, bearing leaves.

Elephants

A busy road, a small field,
a corner of my mind –
three elephants
from Circus Vegas
rock gently, shifting
their wonderful weight
from one foot to another,
chewing their cud.

Here's also a great estate,
a crone in a cave
and bones, extinction
hanging from wires, all
antlers, eye sockets
and fleshless nostrils,
in the long winter of ancient
forest, sycamore and oak.

Here's all this and something else
I haven't quite made out.

When I am old

I'll have dewlaps and a hump and say *what* all the time
in a cross voice: on every one of my bony crony fingers,
a ring. My lips painted with a slash of bright fuchsia,
I'll drink margaritas by the tumbler full and if my dealer
dies before I do, I'll just have to look for younger suppliers.
I can't imagine not being interested in sex, but if it happens,
so be it, really I could do with a rest, complete hormonelessness.
I may forget who I am and how to find my way home, but be
patient, remember I've always been more than a little confused
and never did have much of a sense of direction. If I'm completely
demented, I'm depending on friends: you know who you are.

Nest

I wake beneath a chestnut tree,
back against bark,
legs stretched out through grass.
Long-fingered leaves drip light
and shade haphazardly: the air
is warm. In front of me, a lake
lies like a mirror, and I break
its surface, wash my face
in its salty, ice-cold water.

My horse is waiting, shaded and patient,
his skin is comfort, his breath green
as he carries me on his back
to the flat stone altar at the forest's heart.
Being dead, I lay myself down on it
thankfully, and the black bird comes,
lifts me to her round high nest.

Inside the egg
I am a cell,
dividing and dividing,
first heartbeat,
shell-filtered light
warm on my lidless eyes
until time comes
and the shell cracks.

My horse is waiting,
bright and patient:
his skin is sunlight
and his breath air.
Amongst the moss
his bones
are white and dry.

In my beak, I lift
his great rib hull,
his long leg bones,
the instrument of his skull,

and in the highest branches
of the tallest tree,
in wind-tossed waves of leaves,
I build my horse's nest, my ship of bones.

from *Miracle Fruit*

(2010)

What John Hunter said to me

You know I lived
in a world of pain:
everyone did.
The best surgeon
was the fastest surgeon,
and I was the fastest:

and the hungriest.
Whatever was strange
in nature, I wanted it.
Try it. Take it apart.
Explain it. Know it.
No boundaries restrained me.
I was the most excellent.

I could fill the steep raked
benches of St Thomas's Hospital
with gentlemen in broadcloth coats
and powdered wigs; they leant
on their gold-topped canes,
straining forward to hear me lecture,
of the mercury and sweating cure
for venereal disease,
or the transplantation of teeth.

I could stand for hours in the cold,
my only company the opened, stinking corpse
before me, and I myself almost motionless,
a pair of forceps and my own open fingers,
picking asunder the connecting fibres
of structure, the heart, the lactating breast,
the organs of reproduction; patient as a prophet,
sure that truth would come and darkness become light.

All the death that passed through my workshop –
human, animal – enabled my vast understanding
of comparative anatomy, of all flesh,

so I could slice fearlessly through life,
remove a leg shattered by gunshot, or fingers
crushed beneath a wheel, or a cancerous breast.
I could crack a chest to repair an aortic aneurism.
By what authority do you judge me? Do you not also
want your surgeon to know his job, to cut well?

The skeleton of the great Irish giant

I

Conceived on the very top
of a very high haystack,
in Little Bridge, County Derry,
by his stout, strong-voiced mother
and his average-sized father,
Charles Byrne grew like a cornstalk
and was the talk of London
for years: could be seen
at the sign of the Hampshire
Hog, for half a crown,
or one shilling for children
and servants in livery.
He too had a voice that sounded
like thunder, but his appearance
was far from wholesome.
He constantly dribbled and spat.

Out of fashion,
his savings stolen,
his limbs always aching
and his drinking
killing him surely,
the surgeons gathered
around the house
where he lay
like harpooners
round a whale.
How he feared
their hunger for him.

When he died,

the fishermen
he had employed
to sink his leaded body
twenty fathoms down
and out of reach
succumbed to the bribes.
Handed the huge corpse over
for five hundred pounds.

In his Earl's Court
menagerie, laboratory,
John Hunter, foremost
of those surgeons
and a true scientist,
cut the Irish giant

into chunks and boiled him
in a great copper kettle.
Water plumping, he kept
the Irish giant bubbling
and simmering for days,
fat skimmed off the top:
prepared the skeleton to hang
in his own famous museum.

Disappointingly, the hung frame,
the articulated bones,
measured in at only seven feet
and seven inches, not the eight
feet four the Irish giant
and his manager
had (fraudulently) claimed –
and furthermore
he wasn't the last of his kind.
There was the other Irish giant
and the Gigantic Twin Brothers
who were also natives of Ireland.

Still, his skeleton was a popular exhibit
in the Hunterian and remains there,
an impressive sight even to this day.

II

What? Bones can't speak.
We are all dumb here
in Mr Hunter's marvellous collection
of morbid anatomy, curiosities
and human misery.
Silent as the grave, we hang or float
in our limbo of glass cases
and jars of formaldehyde, darkness
forbidden to us, constantly on show.
We are the blunt truths of the flesh;
what further story do you expect
from me or my twisted companion
bought for eighty-five guineas,
Mr Jaffs, with his *fibrodysplasia
ossificans progressiva*;

or from all the unnamed,
the sliced and the hacked,
from the part of the face
of a child with smallpox,
from the penis and bladder
of a small boy, the skull
of an old woman
who has lost all her teeth,
the breast with a large carcinoma,
the rectum with haemorrhoids,
the femur fractured by gunshot,
the foetuses, the vagina, the femoral artery?
Expendable, all of us, voiceless in death
as in life, we serve to illustrate. What?

Mrs Frame

A Horse-Courser's Wife,
lately living in Barbican,
was afflicted with a swelling
for which she was tapped
and at two tappings
had sixteen gallons of water
let out of her.

She thought – when the Disease
first came upon her
about eleven years ago –
that she was with child
and would not be persuaded
to the contrary ever since.

Just before she died,
at St Bartholomew's Hospital,
she earnestly desired to be opened,
and accordingly, when the Surgeons
had made an incision of her womb,
they found therein the skeleton of a child,
the bones whereof were knitted all together
in their due proportion, but all the flesh thereof
perished and consumed by its immersion in so much water.

Notes taken in the Hunterian

the Animals – 24th October 2009

'John Hunter takes in everything'
Peter Camper Dutch anatomist

disturbing and random
no interest in taxonomy

network of collectors
former students
travellers, naturalists
naval officers
merchants of trading companies

copper boiler in an outhouse

tours for ladies and gentlemen

intestine of a pelican
colon of a lion
fallopian tube of a bottle-nosed whale
foetus of a rhesus monkey
hand and head of a young chimp
'half beast half human'

humerus of a swan
vagina of a minky whale
tip of an elephant's tongue
lower jaw of a golden eagle
brain of a crocodile
from a private menagerie
a grey seal's nose
liver of an opossum
liver of a camel

ovaries of a Surinam toad
a large pregnant African scorpion

and on and on
including the results
of the experimental transplant
of a human tooth
into a cockerel's comb

all the product of his
'virtuous labour'
demonstrating
his 'genius and ardent zeal'

The sow-gelder

He was in the company of several other married men
over a pot or two of ale, when they all joined
in complaint of the fruitfulness of their wives, and asked
could he not spay their wives as he did other animals.
He said he could, and they all agreed their good women
should undergo the operation, provided he would begin
with his own. This with a great oath he undertook.

At home, by violence he bound and gagged his wife
and laying her on the table, made a transverse incision
on the side of her belly, but after much puzzling,
he found there was some difference between the situation
of the parts in the rational and irrational animals, and so,
sewing up the wound, he was forced to give up the experiment.

At the late Assizes held in Bridgewater,
his wife refused to prosecute,
acknowledged her forgiveness of him,
and desired the court would do the same.

Bone voices: Earl's Court

We are a very minor pit of bones;
a pit of very minor bones: the poor,
the won't-be-missed,

tinker, tailor, soldier,
beggar woman, thief,
the pregnant servant girl
who swallowed arsenic,

brought by cart for burial
from the dissecting room
in Castle Street,
delivered at night
through the iron gate
and the drawbridge
that allows access
to the underground yard
of Jack Tearguts.

We know there are pits of bones
everywhere, everywhere
bones and bones and bones,

metacarpals, vertebrae, empty
ribs and skulls that once were
women, children, men,

we taste their numbers
and their silence
in the earth, in the particles

of dirt that pack our jaws.
None of us have any say
in the matter: never have.

An experiment on a bird in an air pump

painting by Joseph Wright of Derby

Hyper-realistic eighteenth-century light, falling
especially to make a point, illuminate a profile;
light that insistently contradicts the darkness,

ranging emotions set out in faces, witnesses
to the birth of science, that precocious, cruel,
self-regarding child with the expendable
dying bird, white cockatoo, exotic marker
of discovery; suffocating, forewarning.

Old gods in the British Museum

They don't cope well
all cooped up together,
so many different persuasions
rubbing shoulders under the one roof.

All uprooted, unworshipped,
held impotent in cold Albion,
fed only the thinnest gruel of awe
from tourists with cameras.

Beneath the impassivity
of their stone faces, they seethe,
or weep, or mutter: some have forgotten
altogether what it was to be feared.

Familiar

So strange and beautiful,
little mummified falcon,
all wrapped up and lain
in the corner of the display case.

I watch you wheel in the sky
that is the same sky, beneath
the sun that is the same sun,
your wings lean on the wind,

and it is as if I have always
known you on my wrist and you
have hunted for me in that life
as you will hunt for me in the next.

Portals

I fell across the doorway, golden heights went on forever,
Anubis weighed my soul as not lighter than a feather.

I fell across the doorway into the open mouth of harm,
the leaves, the leaves all whispering of the approaching storm.

I fell across the doorway, everything was black and red,
the Prince of the Lilies picked me up, carried me to bed.

Crazy Daisy

Our thin-nosed collie who saw visions in the air
and was mad as a god, tapped with her paw
at our living room window the night after she died,
as she always did when she wanted in: we heard,
but couldn't find the door that would admit her.

Becoming an ascetic

It was Diogenes the Cynic who suggested it to me,
the barrel; showed me the very one, a wine cask,
oak and iron, made by a skilled cooper, a thing
of beauty in itself and capable of holding me.

I climb down inside, crouch; the curve fits my spine
perfectly, my legs a tent, knees against my chest.
When I lift my head, stretch my neck back
and look up, I see that stars in daylight also shine.

The year of the great winter

Nearly all the birds died.
Fish froze in the rivers,
animals froze in the forests.
Trees exploded and game
lay down in the fields and died.

Wine froze in the barrels
and it took an axe to cut the bread.

Breath was transformed
into a shower of ice crystals,
falling from mouths
with a tinkling sound,
like the whispers of stars.

How to feed your lover

Starter – Ortolan

First catch your songbird, blind it,
Force-feed it millet, grapes and figs,
then drown the tiny creature in Armagnac,
de-feather and roast for a few minutes
in its own juices; place the embroidered
napkin over your lover's head, to shield her
from the gaze of God and serve her
this two ounces of life, place it hot
on her tongue, only the beak protruding
from her lips: the aromas will fill her senses.
See if she can taste the entire life of the bird,
and, fixed between the last air and the Armagnac,
the flavour of guilt, see if she can cease to exist
except as taste itself, as the small bones lacerate
her gums, as she bites down and chews,
her own blood mixing with the bird's flesh.

Main Course – Blowfish

Buy your fish from the market
where they are sold alive
with their mouths stitched shut.
Slice the flesh thinly, and tenderly
prepare a fine dish of sashimi.
The fish's skin can be puffed up
with air and used as a lantern
for gentle illumination of the feast,
then see if she will trust you enough
to eat; that even when her lips begin
to tingle and become numb,

she'll trust you have not served up
the poison to which there is no antidote.

Dessert – Miracle Fruit

This may prove difficult to source –
you may need to send to the ends
of the earth – but all that is needed
is a sliver of this mythic fruit.
It is well worth the expense and effort,
for once she has eaten it, you will
forever taste of violets in her mouth.

The opening-of-the-mouth ceremony

Seventy days after death, begin the ritual,
place my body in a standing position,
facing south, have a close member of my family
burn incense: the women should wail
and priests attend, foremost
the jackal-masked impersonator of Anubis,
and Ptah, skullcapped dwarf god
who brought all things into being
by thinking of them and saying them with his tongue.

Place my possessions in the tomb –
my bed, my favourite chair and my laptop,
my clothes, jewellery, make-up and perfume,
the foreleg of a sacrificial calf, spurting fresh blood.

Then chant the potent spells, touch my lips with the adze,
metal of heaven that has split open the mouths of the gods.

*

Present me to the child who loves me, who will touch
my mouth with her little finger, as at birth her mouth
was cleaned: so I will have life in the hereafter.

My wandering womb

I stand up
it climbs the ladder of my spine, lodges
itself at the base of my brain.

I lie down
it crawls along my windpipe to crouch
at the back of my throat –

such vagrancy!

Like an animal within an animal
it is altogether erratic: is it any wonder
that I feel panicky, slightly hysterical even.

Deep space and Caroline

When I was a small child, my father
showed me an eclipse of the sun
in a bucket of water.
I would lie awake at night
listening to my brothers
Jacob and William arguing,
over Leibriz and Newton
and the new mathematics
of gradients and curves.

I felt the aftershock
from the Lisbon earthquake
when I was five,
and felt it once more
when I was seventeen, stood
by my father's deathbed.

My face scarred by smallpox,
my growth stunted from typhus,
my destiny was to be the housekeeper,
the spinster, the family's maid,

but I wore a gag to learn to sing

and at twenty-one I watched constellations
from the top of a post-chaise, moving
across Europe, accompanied
by my beloved brother William
and by the rhythm of horse's hooves
and the beat-beat-beat of my heart
escaping.

*

I will learn English
I will run a milliner's shop
and host William's salons.
I will sing for our supper.
I will be full of dreams
and longings

I will help in the grinding
of the mirrors, sometimes
sixteen hours at a stretch
in the stone-flagged basement
among the tools and chemicals
and the horse-dung moulds.
I will keep my brother nourished
by placing the food into his mouth.
I will read to him, relieve the tedium
of the polishing that cannot stop
lest the metal mist, become useless.
I will be his 'boy', his assistant.

I will sit with him and take notes
of his all-night stellar measurements
and observations, together
we will mind the heavens.

I will practise seeing for myself

and with my hunter's telescope
I will sweep the skies
methodically
and find my comet.

I will fall into the night
where there is nothing

to save us
from knowing
our infinite smallness.

I will destroy all my journals
that speak of personal things.

Portrait of my brother as an oxbow lake

Water that has forgotten the flow

that now turns in on itself

choked

still

cut off from me

only visible over my shoulder

Memento

Here: let me give you this crumpled dress,
this rainy night, this moth cocoon,
the voice on the other end of the phone.

Take this small misunderstanding,
this word not spoken, the touch withheld
and the touch given, the hawk's wing.

Have them, the grains of sand,
the full-blown rose, the horse's footfall
and the candlelight, this book of rules;

all strung together, necklaced around
your throat, remembrance, fastened
by a smooth white stone, a twist of hair.

Dunluce Avenue

At each evening's return
you hold the key ready,
push the light switch in
and race the timer two flights
to your bedsit before the hall
and stairs are taken over again
by darkness. This is a house
of dingy melancholy, you're
spooked by it, wish you'd
never moved here, you're
lonely here; it's all wrong.

Be reassured: thirty years from now,
you will have forgotten most things
about this place; no memory
remaining of furniture, décor,
the particular fear,

but you will remember
the professor of Japanese,
elderly and rumpled, soft
as a feather pillow and sad
as a lost empire; his footsteps
across the floor above
in the long hours before dawn.
How you used to wait
for the knock on your door.
Open it; he will be there
holding a jar of warm sake.

A woman addresses her body

For all my talk of soul, it was you
always, sweet little beast, amoral
animal, who showed me the ways
of Love, its passions and crucifixions.

The artist, the anatomist, the poet
and the surgeon, they have seen
the glory in you; you beatified them
in the moments where they believed.

You are my way, my truth, my life;
I am what you have made of me
and still I do not know the limits of you,
or where you will take me next.

Barr Hall

I

This shoreline's stones hold information
in the lines that run and angle through them,
in the circles and swirls: soft through hard,
laid down by time, translated by the sea,
encrypted by tides and fractals of erosion.

What manner of man, when he asked for bread?
I keep my eyes down among the stones, sure
that if I look well enough, I'll find the one
that holds the message for me, understand
what's written there, as it was in the child's eyes.

II

After three days it's getting that I feel I nearly
know this house. I know where the dead spider is,
I know how to draw the blinds, how to lock the door,
and the quality of the mornings: I know how to lie awake.

I've never heard the sound of seals before,
the bluster, cough and wet rasp of their voices.
I watch the tall-masted ship cross the Barr
and it does not feel as if everything I notice
has been noticed before, though the seagulls
mock that thought, raucous as drunks.

I have been too anxious, running after meaning:
let the images dance where circumferences touch,
where the overlap occurs, where the meteors
shower like golden coins burning through blue
before being extinguished in the hissing waves.

III

Among the calls of gulls and curlews,
where mullet mill in the shallows
and my feet have a rhythm on the stones,
I am peaceful and at ease.

The distant, constant Mournes,
the peninsula with its familiar litany
of names, townlands and villages:
Ballywhiskin, Kircubbin, Glastry,

Cardy, Ballywalter, Ards,
cartography of my childhood, of my life.
This is my home, this small acreage,
and for the first time, I feel at home

now that so much has dropped away
and I want less and I want more.
A colder madness holds me in the stillness
of Cuan, my lough of safe haven.

Alone

If I lived by myself
I would be careful about things,
I wouldn't burn to death
because of the candle
forgotten.

I'd get more sleep,
my washing would
always be done
and my correspondence
up to date.

I'm not sure how much I would drink
or smoke:
it could be less
or it could be more.
I'd eat better.

Gladioli

How glad I am that months ago, I planted
the bulbs whose growth I harvest now
against our too early, low-skied autumn.

Lustful, affirmative, they move this evening
to a different place just by being on the windowsill
in their white vase, the evening blue behind them.

Vigorous spears, I hear their colour behind my eyes,
jubilant life, rebounding off the bone, bouncing
chamber to chamber and on through every artery and vein.

Grief

If I were to write
another poem
about grief,
it would be full
of the absences
of animals –

Kitty, Dilly, Pip and Daisy,
Sezmo, Princess, Baby –

each small loss
another lesson: every
thing we love will go away.

31st January

I want to be somewhere
else; out of this greyness
and in amongst heat, colour;
orange, olive, terracotta, red,
where even the yellow stone
is warm from holding the sun

and only the white marble,
quarried from darkness,
is cool, and just the right
coolness against my skin,
my skin that tingles with
heat and light full of gold,

where even the night is warm
and scented with lemon
and I will sit outside,
supper on bread and olives,
apricots and walnuts, stars,
bare arms and summer's wine.

Balances

It is the longest day,
the orange sunset on the black horizon balances
the orange moon rising through black clouds;
one horse is the shadow of the other, light
and dark are in my heart; I am equidistant
from north and south, east and west.
Three hundred and sixty degrees
I have surrounded myself with guardians:
gods and dragon dogs and multitudes of birds.
The wind still worries at me though;
it comes from all directions, changeable,
finding every crack in my defences,
laying low all manner of things, my rest,
my senses, my delicate blossoms –
I will plant only what can survive.

Learning the way

The mice have their ways
through the house, along
the pipes, through the gaps
in floorboards,
to anywhere they want.

Listen,
at night
the mothers
leading the little ones
along the ways of the house

so that next year,
when the weather
turns cold, the new
generation will know
how to inhabit our space.

*

We've had enough of tiny teeth
gnawing through our dreams,
pellets of shit in the hot press,
incessant scratching behind the walls,

so each night we set the traps
and each morning there is
a mother's body to be disposed of,
in the bin, neck snapped.

After a week, ten days,
the smell begins to sickly, sweetly
rise from under the floorboards,
from the nests, from the unfed dead pups

Beekeeper

sends me a gift, a tiny cage
of silver filigree and bone,
scalpel-carved,

inside the cage
a single honey bee,
buzzing with entrapment.

That night I dream
of a mossy bed, blue
bells, honey dripping

onto a veil, my mouth
stung, my lips swelling,
my voice gone.

Doubt

The next day is stormy and the coast
has changed: silver light, silver waves.
His hair is silver, coarse like the pelt
of an animal, a seal lifting its wet head
through the sea: me on the wild shore.

How far away I feel, how forsaken
by the god I don't believe in: and by
this saviour that speaks in tongues
of fire and flesh and poetry, lying
as I lie, embraced in a worn-out faith.

Solar lanterns

As night falls, they hold a vestige of the sun;
enough to shine among the garden's late green,
like candles lit for safe return: like the candles
I have lit in churches and cathedrals,
cities and towns I happen to be tourist in,
struck against my unbelief and for my dead.
Just little lights, not much against the dark.

Man-bear in London, 1720

We have a very odd creature here,
like a man in shape,
but furred like a bear.
They tell us he came from Ireland,
where he lived till he was twenty
and ran wild in the woods.

All the parts of his body
are overgrown with long black hair,
which they have stiffened and rubbed backwards:
makes him look very deliciously, it seems,
and the women go in shoals to see him.

They show him for two-pence a piece
and an innumerable many customers they have had;
but as they expose him no lower than his waist,
their trade begins to fail them,
and the females' curiosity to abate.

Mary Patterson

Plied with gin, stupefied,
Burke's knee on my breast,
Hare's hand across my breath
till the life is pressed out of me,
then I'm delivered to your door

and it was one thing Dr Knox,
who buys the beef,
to take my body,
for professional
scientific purposes,
for the greater good,
so to speak,

and for certain my body
was worth more as dead meat –
I'd hitch up my skirts
for just a few coins
in the shadows of Canongate,
whereas you paid seven pounds
and ten shillings –

but to lay me out like that,
naked on the couch,
sensuously arranged
under the flickering candlelight,
my dead face seductively
turned to the audience,
and a white sheet draped
teasingly over my calves,

and then have me sketched
before my dissection –

now that's a disgrace.
What were you thinking?

And you, Mr Ferguson, surgeon
in training, looking at me,
in your professional capacity

as I looked at you in mine
just two nights previous.
You still want to use me?

Hogarth self-portrait with pug

Who is this and what is she doing here
like a distorting mirror, looking at me
as if I am not me but her? A different time,
but still with my pug beside me and still
gin lane, the four stages, the marriage à la

mode. I've been kind to myself, but she knows
how it is: outside it is raining and as the needle
disappears into the grey sky, the same things
are happening that have always happened,
and nothing is so black and white that it is

not lived in vividness. I'm only part of this,
and so is she, and those she's with, the figures
beside her, behind her, inside her, jostling,
casting a shadow backwards to what lies
before us all, and the whole lineup of us

know it's about flesh, its influence, the demands
it makes upon us, its hungers and requirements;
how it makes us who we are, despite our desire
to be something lighter: it holds us to ourselves.
Ballast to our souls, vain blood looks through.

Balloon

What an absolutely wonderful day.
I was dressed of course for the occasion:
a new dress, the bodice cut low
to show my magnificent breasts
to best advantage,
and the silk, a deep red
to compliment
the swags of heavier silk
that draped the wicker gondola.

So in we clambered, Mr Lunardi,
young Mr Biggin the Old Etonian,
and me – Mrs Sage – actress
and First Ever Aerial Female.

There was a teensy problem then.
Mr Lunardi had been
too much the gentleman
to enquire how much I weighed,
so had miscalculated.
Gallantly, he exited the basket,
leaving it light enough to rise,
and leaving me and the lovely
rich young man
to soar without him.

I had to get down on all fours
to do up the gondola's lacing,
so I'm afraid the people of Piccadilly
had a view of my large
but rather delectable bottom.
Lord knows what they thought
I was doing, and gorgeous George

(we were on first-name terms
by then) did get rather overwrought –
I couldn't help but notice.
Then of course I trod
on the barometer,
so we couldn't actually tell
what heights we'd reached,

but other than that, well
we had a simply wonderful time.
We had Italian sparkling wine
and cold chicken
and called to the people below
though a speaking trumpet.

The views were magnificent
and I had no need whatsoever
of my smelling salts.

We landed at Harrow on the Hill
in an unharvested hayfield; unfortunately,
the farmer was a complete savage,
yelling and swearing most inappropriately
and accusing us of ruining his crop.
Thankfully we were rescued
by a delightful young gentleman
from Harrow School
who, as I'd hurt a tendon in my foot,
carried me to the local tavern,
where we all got wonderfully drunk.

I did hear that in Mr Biggin's London club
there was a deal of speculation
as to what else we might have engaged in
up there in the heavens; cries of
Did he board her? There's men for you.

I suppose that when I go out now
I shall be much looked at,

as if a native of the Aerial Regions
had come down to pay an earthly visit.

How to make a pig-faced woman

First start a rumour, such as that started
about poor weathy Gizel Steevens of Dublin: pious
and charitable, she paid for the building of a hospital,
but also wore a veil and was of a retiring disposition.

Then write a pamphlet – A True Description
of the Young Lady Born with the Face of a Pig.
Bind the slim volume in pigskin for special effect.
Put on show the silver trough from which she eats her gruel.

Next procure a black bear and drug with warm strong ale.
Shave its snout, neck, paws; lug to a comfortable chair
and dress in a lady's costume with padded bosom, frills and ribbons.
Satin gloves for the front paws, elegant shoes for the rear,
a large wig, blonde and ringletted, a fashionable hat on top.

Are you the heiress to a large fortune? Poke. Grunt.
Do you feed from a silver trough? Poke. Grunt.

Poor rich Gizel, horrified that the populace of Dublin
had turned her into a pig-faced woman – boys grunting
at her in the street, men jumping on the footstep of her carriage
to catch a glimpse of her snout – sat out on her balcony
with her perfectly ordinary face in full view and had her portrait
painted and hung in the hospital halls. To no avail.
Everyone knew Madame Steevens had the face of a pig.

Because you're worth it, *circa* 1772

Fashion is infinitely superior to merit.
Josiah Wedgewood

Even as a child I had beautiful hands,
not pudgy like my older sister's, whose fingers
couldn't stretch past half an octave on the piano keys.
My fingers are long and slender and elegant,
the perfect setting for the jewelled rings
my husband has bought and given to me.
I see him watch their gracefulness, my hands
and wrists, as I move them to smooth my skirts,
undo a button, or let down my hair.

Sometimes I catch a glimpse of Cook's hands,
fingers like half-boiled sausages, lumpen
and misshapen; or the parlour maid's, red
and chapped, so rough it makes me feel quite ill.
I shudder even thinking about hands like those.

I couldn't bear to live with hands like those.
This year's new product, an arsenic mixture
specifically for hands, to whiten them,
was recommended to me by a friend.
I use it every day and it is marvellously
efficacious: my hands grow paler by the week,

and then, in Mr Wedgewood's showroom,
Portland Lane, I see the most divine new range
of tea sets, specifically designed to compliment
the whiteness of a lady's hands. I had to have one.
Now, when visitors call, the teapot's basalt blackness
allows me to show the beauty of my alabaster fingers

to wonderful effect. I see them look –
though lately I have felt lethargic, a little nauseous,
with stomach cramps, and in all honesty
not enjoying company as much as once I did:
I do hope I am not becoming ill.

Sabrina

There is absolutely no need to feel sorry for me.
It worked out very well: I became Mrs Bicknell,
and John was a good man – not that Mr Day wasn't.

Strange, yes, with his philosophy and notions, and yes,
a bit cruel when you look at it from the point of view
of a twelve-year-old girl,
which is what I was when he picked me.

Still, he kept his word and without him
I might have ended up on the streets; most likely would,
for what else could I have done, an orphan with no one?

I sense your disapproval: well, maybe you live
in different times and there are no poor children
to be exploited, no small boys are crippled
by being sent up chimneys; no children
starve to death, no babies get left outside to die,

and no rich person could just arrive at a foundling hospital
to choose a little girl to take home with them,
to do with what they wish – but that's how it was
when I lived, and it could have been worse for me:
it can always be worse.

Mr Day was a disciple of Rousseau, and too deeply earnest,
so they said, to submit to the ordinary compromises of society,
which was why he determined on his experiment
to train a girl to be the perfect wife: high-virtued,
courageous, with a taste for literature, science and philosophy,
but with the simplest of tastes in clothes, food and way of life.
She should be prepared to live calmly, in seclusion, and in total
obedience to her husband. Of course I knew nothing of this

the day they lined up us girls, the ones just approaching
    womanhood,
but still innocent, and he walked up and down, looking at us.

He stopped in front of me and I looked up from below my eyelids,
saw a tall man, heavy-jawed with a tangle of dark hair.
This child seems suitable, he said in his clear voice. Later,
after he'd taught me to read, I used to think he talked like a book,
but on that day I understood little of his fancy words, before I
knew it
I was parcelled up and put onto the coach with him, lurching
through the dark, cold and afraid, Shrewsbury to London,
where he picked another girl, dark-haired, a nice contrast
to my own flaxen locks, but the same age as me. Two of us:
twice the chance for success. He named her Lucretia: me
he called Sabrina, and that's what I've been known as ever since.

I was so sick on the ship to France I thought
I was like to die – and wanted to.
By the time we got to Avignon I hated her,
with her constant whining and complaining
and always trying to get me into trouble.

He did his best to educate us
in the severest of principles
so that we would acquire
the strength of mind he required
in a wife. We were wild little things,
though, fought and scrapped,
biting and kicking and hair-pulling.
At least I learnt to read – not like her,
who couldn't even do that.
By the time we moved back to England
he'd given up on her, called her
invincibly stupid, which she was,

but good to his word he placed her
with a milliner as an apprentice.
I heard she married a linen draper,
so she did all right too: I told you
he wasn't a bad man. He kept on
with me, trying to shape me
to his satisfaction, and not succeeding.
When he dropped melted sealing wax
onto my arm, I just couldn't keep quiet.
I squealed, and pulled my arm away.
When he fired pistols round my feet
and at my petticoats, I have to confess
I screamed, and cursed him; when
he tested my reticence, I found
I couldn't keep a secret either, so that
was that, I was out of the running
to be his wife and sent to boarding school.
He was a good man, he could have
just turned me out onto the streets.

I heard the woman he did marry,
Esther, when he made her walk
barefoot in the snow, wept
but did not complain, and that
is what he appears to have wanted.

I was sorry enough when I heard he had died.
When he tried to break the spirit of a horse
the creature threw him on his head.

Bruising Peg

At Hockey in the Hole, or in the Amphitheatre
where cocks and bulls and Irish women fight,
I fought

the vendor of sprats from Billingsgate,
the ass driver from Stoke Newington,
the Newgate Market basket woman
the Hiberian Heroine
the Championess of the City,

and I pulverised them all: my physical capital
no less than any man's. I am weapon and target,
bare-knuckled, bare-breasted, my hair tied up,
and a half-pint of gin in me, I fear nothing and no one.
Let the bets be laid and the blood begin. Come on.

Jolly Daisy

We were having a hard season, wet weekends,
cold winds, and farmers too worried 'bout their crops
to go to carnival; worst of all, we didn't have a freak.
We'd a good enough show. I did a bit of fire-eating
and sword-swallowing, Krinko hammered nails
up his nose, Captain Billy did the Bed of Pain,
and the Human Ostrich swallowed mice, brought
them up again still wriggling: all the kind of stuff
anyone would enjoy – but we badly needed a freak.

The night I first saw Jolly Daisy, she staggered in
wheezing and puffing, her fluffy pink dress soaked
with sweat, her thick legs barely able to support
the great mass of her body. Well, I thought,
it's not the original Siamese twins but it'll do.

Leave me lie down.

Three of us supported her to the bed,
where she collapsed, a mountain of exhausted flesh.
The four legs of the bed sank into the wet earth of the top.
Her dress had ridden up over her vast thighs.

I think I'm dying,
this time I'm dying for sure.

We had our freak.

*

Me and him, the fire-eater,
we get to talking between shows.
I show him a picture of my kid.

You have a child, *all surprised,*
Is she . . . ? *No, I tells him,*
she ain't fat like me, she's normal.
It ain't wise, though,
for her to know that I'm her mother.
The nuns send me pictures.

Men ain't no good.
I'd be a faithful wife
to a decent man: sure a wife
ought to help her husband some,
but sometimes he ought
to make some money for hisself.
The one I left to come here,
I have to give him due,
he was a good talker.
A good talker
can point an act up nicely.
He used to get fifteen
minutes of comedy out of me –
like he'd drop a coin,
tell me to pick it up,
and when I bend over,
my skirt rides up so high
it shows my arse, that
gives the crowd a laugh.
Krinko just says – This
is Jolly Daisy,
the fattest lady in the world –
and the tip looks and passes by.

I'll stay till the end of the season,
then move on
to one of the big city's dime museums.

How to swallow a sword

There are over two hundred names
in the Sword Swallower's Hall of Fame –
and that's not counting the fakirs,
the Greeks and Romans, the Mayan Indians,
the Chinese, the Japanese or the Sufis.

There is Signor Wandana, Professor Pierce,
the Mighty Ajax, Chief Willie Bowlegs,
The Great Zadma, Skippy the Clown
and Edith Clifford, Champion
Sword Swallower of the World,
taught the skill at thirteen
by one-legged Delmo Fritz.

Begin with something short –
a pair of scissors
or a paper knife –
learn to control
your gag reflex, that involuntary
reaction that arises in the nerves,

keep a bowl beside you
until you have conditioned yourself
to do what your defence mechanisms
try to prohibit,

teach your upper gastro-
intestinal tract to relax
tilt your head back
extend the neck
align the mouth
with the oesophagus

move the tongue aside
line up the sword
and move it
through the mouth
pharynx past
the sphincter muscle.

On its way down
the sword straightens out
oesophageal curves
nudges the heart aside
enters the stomach.

Edith, employed by Barman and Bailey,
was fêted in the Royal Courts of Europe
(Houdini said) for her more-than-ordinary
personal charms, her refined taste in clothes
and her unswerving devotion to her art.

Blades of twenty inches
without a problem, sometimes ten
or sixteen at a time.

Two marriages,
Thomas, the Elastic Stretch Man,
and after him, Karl the Trapeze Artist,
then retirement, to open her grocery store.

Her grandson does not remember her
ever speaking of her show-business career
and never saw her swallow a sword,
though he has kept one in a cupboard at his home
and can be persuaded to pose with it for the camera.

Youth riding

after Picasso

I will both remember and forget
how easy it is and how light I am;
the smell of the trodden earth
in the big ring, sweat and perfume
of the crowd. It was never just an act.
See me, my hair flowing behind me,
my body obliviously balanced
on the moment's broad back.

Dissolution of the circus

After the last of the big cats died,
toothless and emaciated, the elephant
was impounded by animal welfare
and the ponies were sold to a riding school,
where they soon forgot all their tricks.
The bearded lady had electrolysis,
married the fat man, who'd joined a gym
and was less than half the man he used to be.
The clown enrolled with the Open University –
English Literature and Philosophy –
and the contortionist gave up cocaine,
finally straightened out his head.
There's only the two of us left now:
me and the ringmaster with his top hat
and his whip, and though the spangles
have mostly fallen off my costume
I can still balance up there on the wire.

Acknowledgements

I would like to thank the Arts Council Northern Ireland for their support through an Artist's Career Enhancement Award. Thanks also to the friends who have provided support and encouragement over the years.

Note

The poems in this collection previously appeared in *Snakeskin Stilettos* (1998), *Beneath the Ice* (2001), *The Horse's Nest* (2006) and *Miracle Fruit* (2010), all published by Lagan Press.